Praise for *The Heart of Money*

"How wonderful to have a practical guide to empower couples to discuss their sensitivities and differences around finances. *The Heart of Money* will assist readers to bring about mutually respectful decisions that will bring satisfaction and fulfillment to all issues related to financial challenges. Whether working co-operatively to generate more income or being content with what we have, the intimacy, trust, and happiness that result from deep understanding is indeed our greatest wealth."

— Linda Bloom, LCSW, coauthor of
101 Things I Wish I Knew When I Got Married
and *Secrets of Great Marriages*

Praise for *Money Magic* by Deborah L. Price

"*Money Magic* can assist you in transforming your consciousness, making you more receptive to the prosperity seeking to flow through you as you live a purposeful life."

— Michael Bernard Beckwith, author of *Spiritual Liberation*

"Going well beyond 'manifesting' money, or 'visualizing prosperity,' *Money Magic* can help readers understand and overcome their lifelong money issues."

— *NAPRA ReView*

"A must-read for creating wealth and understanding our often precarious relationship with money. Deborah Price has created a handbook that encompasses everything the reader would need to gain both prosperity and peace of mind."

— Benjamin Shield, PhD, editor of
Handbook for the Soul and *Handbook for the Spirit*

"Drawing on her own experience as well as her counseling practice, Price describes the eight types of relationships people have with money and outlines how one can become a 'money Magician,' bringing one's attitude toward money in better alignment with deeper life goals."

— *Publishers Weekly*

"Read this book and watch your wealth bounce higher! Deborah Price is right on the money!"

— Roger Crawford, author of *How High Can You Bounce?*

"Savor the down-to-earth insights [*Money Magic*] gives you into your relationship with money."

— *Spirituality & Health*

The Heart of Money

Also by Deborah L. Price

*Money Magic: Unleashing Your True Potential
for Prosperity and Fulfillment*

Start Investing Online Today!

The Heart of Money

*A Couple's Guide
to Creating
True Financial Intimacy*

Deborah L. Price

New World Library
Novato, California

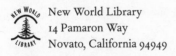 New World Library
14 Pamaron Way
Novato, California 94949

Text design by Tona Pearce Myers

Library of Congress Cataloging-in-Publication Data
Price, Deborah L., date.
The heart of money : a couple's guide to creating true financial intimacy / Deborah L. Price.
    p.   cm.
Includes bibliographical references and index.
ISBN 978-1-60868-127-3 (pbk. : alk. paper)
1. Married people—Finance, Personal. 2. Couples—Finance, Personal.
3. Finance, Personal—Psychological aspects. 4. Money—Psychological aspects. 5. Man-woman relationships. I. Title.
HG179.P7353 2012
332.0240086'55—dc23   2012024309

First printing, October 2012
ISBN 978-1-60868-127-3
Printed in Canada on 100% postconsumer-waste recycled paper

 New World Library is proud to be a Gold Certified Environmentally Responsible Publisher. Publisher certification awarded by Green Press Initiative. www.greenpressinitiative.org

10 9 8 7 6 5 4 3 2 1

To my daughter, Anjelica Price-Rocha,
and my husband, Robert Coleman,
who have both taught me the true meaning of love.

Passion can never purchase what true love desires:
true intimacy, self-giving, and commitment.

— AUTHOR UNKNOWN

CONTENTS

ACKNOWLEDGMENTS

I have been enormously blessed in my life with the gift of the most wonderful circle of loving and supportive friends and family. These are the people whom I know I can count on in this world, who always have my back, and without whom my life would simply not be the same. My heartfelt gratitude goes out to the following people.

My daughter, Anjelica Price-Rocha, for her wisdom and great writing and editing skills. My husband and best friend, Robert Coleman, for his unconditional support, editorial assistance, and honest feedback as my "in-house editor."

My business partner and friend, Steven "Shags" Shagrin, for tirelessly reading my drafts and providing friendship, editing, and support throughout.

My wonderful girlfriends: Marian Morioka and Carol Bell, who fed me, loved me, and provided endless entertainment throughout; and Donna Colfer, Karen Harvey, and Molly Light, for being such dear friends and bearers of love and light in my world.

Leslie Gainer, for her friendship, wisdom, and perspective just when I needed them most.

Lili Goodman-Freitas and Greg Freitas, for the love, light, and laughter they brought into our lives.

Dr. and Mrs. Preston and Frieda Wright, for always knowing what to say and do to make it better.

Marge Abrams, Stephan Islas, Brenda Ferreira, and David Seligman, for always being there for me for as long as I can remember.

Janet Rosen and Sheree Bykofsky, for being the best agents a writer could ever hope for.

And finally, love and gratitude to my editor, Georgia Hughes, and New World Library, for continuing to believe in me and support my ideas.

FOREWORD

As a licensed clinical psychologist, I began my relationship with Deborah Price and the Money Coaching Institute with a certain amount of skepticism. Here was a woman with no formal psychological training tackling the biggest taboo subject in the world: money and our relationship to it. Her first book, *Money Therapy: Using the Eight Money Types to Create Wealth and Prosperity*, claimed to help people to transform their relationship with money not only from a practical perspective but also through sound psychological principles so that they could lead more purposeful and prosperous lives. As I read, I quickly shed my skepticism, and over the past five years of knowing and working with Deborah, I have become increasingly respectful of and impressed by her deep wisdom and skill in working with clients as a money coach. Deborah is a highly experienced teacher and coach with a remarkable ability to communicate complex information so that it can be easily digested and practically implemented to effect significant change.

In my training as a psychologist and throughout my work in the field, I have been amazed by the lack of focus given to the emotional impact that money has on our lives. Therapists are typically not trained to work with clients on their relationship with money and often feel afraid to address this issue. Similarly, most financial experts have neither the knowledge nor the training to work with clients on the qualitative issues of money, discussing their feelings, their fears, or their unconscious patterned behaviors. Remarkably, open discussion of finances and money choices rarely happens even in our most intimate and trusted relationships, with our partners. Despite the importance, there is a huge vacuum in exploring our relationship with money, what motivates our money behaviors, and the unconscious choices we often make with regard to how we use money. This reality has impacted our current financial situation, on both a micro- and macrolevel, with the result that money is the leading cause of divorce and whole countries are now threatened with bankruptcy.

Money is consistently the number one thing that couples fight about, regardless of where they fall on the socioeconomic spectrum. This is not surprising given the lack of infrastructure we have around discussing money. Any topic that cannot be openly examined, giving people the opportunity to consciously think about what their values and goals are, what messages and rules they have inherited, and how they want to consciously act, is subject to blind, unexamined reaction. Shoot-from-the-hip interactions with money do not serve individuals, couples, families, communities, or our global society and have a tremendous ripple effect.

It is time to banish this taboo and begin to have open discussions about money. Weaving a masterful understanding of human behavior and motivation with hands-on expertise in creating and sustaining financial success, Deborah Price is a maverick and a pioneer in the field, bringing forward a comprehensive body of work that has been missing from both the field of psychology and the financial planning and advisory fields. Her books and professional trainings through the Money Coaching Institute provide a step-by-step process for identifying, understanding, and transforming one's relationship with money in order to achieve greater financial awareness and prosperity.

Successful interaction with money requires an ability to quickly assess a situation and consciously utilize the most beneficial archetype to take effective action. To do this, we must learn about the characteristics of the various archetypes that Deborah Price describes in her book as well as our particular money histories to become aware of our conditioned patterns of interacting with money and how to consciously shift to more advantageous behaviors. We also need to be able to deftly understand which archetypes are showing up in other people's actions around money and then manage our own behaviors in a way that achieves positive outcomes. This is the brilliance of *The Heart of Money*. In this book, Deborah Price recognizes the relationship between couples as a primary one and helps them to work together toward financial transparency and intimacy, powerfully strengthening their relationship and efficacy in interacting with money. Incorporating the Money Coaching Institute's archetypal model in our work at the Wealth Legacy Group, we have seen significant shifts in results with clients. Couples have worked together more effectively in ways that were astonishingly simple yet powerful to transform their dynamics as they related to money.

For each individual and couple who reads this book and takes more conscious actions around money, there will be an exponential positive impact in how families, communities, and ultimately our global economy interact with money. I thank you in advance for contributing to this much-needed change.

Jamie Traeger-Muney, PhD
Founder, Wealth Legacy Group

INTRODUCTION

Money, love, sex... any one of these subjects represents a plethora of complex emotions and experiences that human beings have grappled with throughout history. When you mix these issues together, you have perhaps the most challenging and combustible material known to humankind. No wonder money issues are a major source of conflict in our relationships! Even in the best of economic times, over 50 percent of all marriages in the United States end in divorce. Given the current economic recession and the mounting financial pressures that couples are experiencing, it is likely that money issues and conflicts will continue to increase, as will the corresponding divorce rates.

The subject of money is still highly taboo and one that people will go to great lengths to avoid. Yet couples who are in a committed relationship or married cannot have a healthy, truly intimate relationship unless they are willing to be financially open and fully transparent about their financial wants, needs, and expectations. Financial intimacy requires the willingness to be self-revealing and vulnerable; to be seen for who we really are; to share our fears and our secrets; and to love and accept one another unconditionally, flaws included. It takes an emotionally and financially mature person to achieve this depth of intimacy. While many people may possess the emotional maturity, relatively few are also financially mature enough to manage this terrain alone. Achieving this level of financial maturity and consciousness is remarkably difficult for most individuals (let alone couples!), which is why we experience so much conflict in our relationships.

When it comes to identifying and changing our money patterns and behaviors, we receive very little help, if any, for understanding ourselves and our money issues. Even most psychologists admit that they are not trained or educated with respect to money issues. And, while the fields of behavioral finance, neuroscience, and neuroeconomics have begun to delve into this arena, any knowledge gained so far is not being utilized in the trenches with real people who are struggling daily to save their relationships and financial lives. At the Money Coaching Institute, we are working to change this dynamic by training hundreds of money coaches worldwide to integrate our programs and to help individuals and couples to heal and change their relationship with money.

Money is a core survival issue. When people are fearful and anxious about money and their personal finances, they are frequently too overwhelmed and stressed to be focused and present. Prolonged financial pressures also lead to increased problems with spouses; alcohol and drug abuse; and, sadly, a corresponding increase in depression, despair, and suicide. According to the Center for Financial Social Work, money issues are

- the number one stressor in people's lives
- the number one cause of divorce

- a major source of depression, anxiety, and insomnia
- a primary reason for abuse and violence
- a trigger for alcohol and drug abuse
- overwhelming and immobilizing
- accompanied by feelings of hopelessness, shame, isolation, and vulnerability
- an emotional roller coaster that diminishes coping and decision-making skills
- a cause of distraction, anger, irritability, mistakes, and accidents.

The bottom line is this: if we do not feel financially safe and secure in our primary relationships, we cannot experience financial intimacy. In order to become truly financially intimate, we must first learn how to openly and honestly communicate about money while safely expressing our hopes, fears, needs, and desires. Without financial intimacy and safety, our relationships lack the foundation required to survive the challenges and experiences that most relationships eventually encounter over time. Thus, at a time when the United States and the world are experiencing major financial meltdowns, relationships are also beginning to experience foundational cracks, and the fallout from both may very well be the worst in history. Even before the current financial debacle, couples were stressed by mounting debt, mortgage foreclosures, and bankruptcies.

When money is scarce, it is easy to become emotionally triggered, which is why many couples are prone to reacting impulsively where money is concerned. When we are highly fearful, the fight-or-flight response system is activated in the brain, which does not bode well for our interpersonal relationships. How can we learn to not abandon ourselves, our families, and our children when both global and personal financial challenges continue to trigger our own deeply unresolved money issues? Our money issues will not change or suddenly disappear simply because our finances improve or even if we decide to leave our relationships. Divorce is often more of a Band-Aid than a solution to money issues. As Confucius said, "No matter where you go, there you are." For many couples, things might in fact get worse, especially for the woman. Women, particularly single mothers, tend to fare significantly worse financially post-divorce than men do. Not that I believe couples should stay married simply for financial security. However, many marriages might possibly be saved if couples were able to resolve their underlying money issues and communicate more calmly and reflectively, rather than reactively.

What the World Needs Now: Money Therapy

The list of "money disorders" seems to be growing by the day. Among the issues we grapple with are compulsive spending, financial infidelity, debt addiction, hoarding, overspending, underspending, money phobia, compulsive gambling, financial enabling, chronic underearning, and workaholism. Because it's a core survival issue, everyone can feel vulnerable when it comes to money. It's also an area of our lives that at times can feel out of control or deeply affected by the actions of others. That we become so easily reactive around money is not surprising when we consider that most people have not been given the proper training or education about money or personal financial matters. How can we feel safe, secure, and confident when we lack the tools we need to make good financial choices and to be financially empowered?

Perhaps it's time for a little money therapy. If we have a

plumbing problem, we don't hesitate to call a plumber. If we have a health problem, we go see the doctor. If we have money issues, we deserve the help and advice of a professional as well. Money affects every aspect of our lives, and yet we know very little about our personal relationship with it. Isn't it time we heal our relationship with money?

As we become more aware of our own money patterns and behaviors, we can begin to make new, healthier choices. This is a great first step toward creating a new financial legacy for ourselves and our children — a legacy built on self-awareness, knowledge, and power instead of stress, fear, mistrust, or dependence. But first we must each begin to understand and heal our own relationship with money.

It is estimated that the combined total of financial casualties since 2008 in the United States alone may exceed 3.5 million by the end of 2012. That means roughly one in every fifty families will be affected by this recession, which is staggering to consider. One thing is certain: if we are to individually and collectively survive, and in fact thrive again, we must confront this final frontier and take the money conversation out of the closet once and for all. It is time to shift our collective money paradigm. Throughout this book, you will discover highly effective strategies and solutions to help you begin the financial healing process and strengthen the intimacy in your relationship. My intention is to provide help and hope for couples and their families everywhere, as I've witnessed the same money issues and dynamics in clients globally. Let this book guide you to discover and work through your money dynamics — and in doing so, live more purposeful and financially empowered lives. I truly believe that when couples develop financial intimacy and can effectively communicate about money, they can communicate about *anything*.

A Note to the Reader

Please note that throughout this book you will see references to God, Source, and Spirit, which I use interchangeably to mean "a Higher Power." Please know that I have no religious agenda in writing this book. Humanity is my religion. How or whether a person believes in God is deeply personal, and I honor that in every human being. My clients come from all walks of spiritual life; they are Christians, Jews, Muslims, Buddhists, Catholics, Sikhs, and Hindis, as well as nonbelievers. They all know that I honor their distinct relationship with God. Spirituality infuses and informs everything I do, and you will hear this echoed throughout these pages. I invite you to take or leave my spiritual perspective as it serves you. It is offered without attachment or agenda.

This book will guide you and your partner to move beyond limiting money patterns and beliefs through exercises designed to help you to safely explore, communicate about, and understand each other's money dynamics. Each chapter in this book includes excerpts and exercises from coaching sessions conducted with actual clients. I suggest that you do this work together and that you both keep a money coaching journal throughout the process. The exercises included in each chapter are designed to help you work together and discuss your experience as you proceed. It is my intention that couples who read this book discover new and healthy ways to communicate safely and effectively around money, love, and relationship. Money can either be left as the unexamined "shadow" or become transformed by our willingness to look deeply into ourselves and take responsibility for our own choices and destiny.

Chapter One

MONEY: THE LAST TABOO

*No failure in America, whether of love or money,
is ever simple; it is always a kind of betrayal,
of a mass of shadowy, shared hopes.*

— GREIL MARCUS, *Mystery Train*

If you look around at the world today, our collective money issues lie somewhere deep at the root of every major global problem we are facing. Unthinkable greed, overconsumption, environmental abuse, mass poverty, outrageous military spending, and the global financial crisis have caused us finally to hit bottom. While waking up from this hangover may not be easy, there has never been a more compelling time to shift our collective relationship with money. The subject of money is the last taboo and the final horizon in the evolution of our human consciousness.

Almost every relationship encounters challenges or outright conflict around money at some point. In my experience, few couples know how to communicate effectively about this highly charged subject in a way that is compassionate and supportive. No wonder many marriages disintegrate and fail over money issues! Issues and conflict around money remain a leading cause of divorce, which leaves in its wake not only financial consequences but emotional devastation as well.

Left unmanaged and without proper and timely help, money issues will eventually chip away at the foundation of trust and intimacy in our relationships. Without trust, intimacy cannot survive, and without intimacy, love withers and dies. The good news is that if couples recognize and manage their money dynamics early in their relationship — or, better yet, before they live together or marry — they can learn how to work through and heal their differences.

How can we do this if we can't even talk about money calmly and rationally because the subject is so taboo, triggering, and unsafe? Therein lies the challenge and what I most hope to assist you with. The money coaching strategies and support in this book will help you to achieve the understanding and compassion you need to foster the love and intimacy you both desire.

Breaking Free of the Money Taboo

According to the *Cambridge Dictionary*, a taboo is "something that is avoided or forbidden for religious or social reasons," and therefore, talking about a taboo subject is often considered wrong or distasteful. In the past sixty years, we've opened the door to exploring many historically taboo subjects, such as sex, ethnicity, religion, and politics; and in doing so, we have expanded and evolved both our individual and our collective consciousness. As a reward for these efforts, we have all witnessed and experienced greater openness, acceptance, and tolerance in the world at large.

Yet somehow, money has remained a vastly unexplored taboo,

and there is more than sufficient evidence to show that this taboo is simply not serving us. The emotional and financial pain and consequences that couples experience are taking a toll and costing them far too much. It is time to break free of the money taboo and heal our collective money issues.

Facing the Money Shadow

Any area of our lives that remains off-limits to talk about openly, honestly, and without fear can become a "shadow" part of our being. In Jungian psychology, the *shadow* or *shadow aspect* represents a part of our unconscious mind that contains repressed aspects of ourselves. Carl Jung wrote that "everyone carries a shadow, and the less it is embodied in the individual's conscious life, the blacker and denser it is." In monetary terms, the shadow represents unconscious money patterns or behaviors we may possess that are harmful to ourselves or to others.

One example of this is when a person secretly invests a large sum of money without the knowledge of his or her partner and then loses the money, creating an extreme financial loss and feelings of betrayal. This has happened with many of the couples in my practice, and in each case, shadow influences were present in the partner who had secretly invested. In one couple, the shadow aspect of the husband had to do with unacknowledged anger toward his wife. Rather than learning how to address and communicate his anger, he acted out his feelings through secret behavior that ultimately sabotaged their finances and their relationship. Fortunately, they were able to heal and resolve this betrayal, but sadly, it doesn't always work out favorably. Many marriages fail due to the shadow influences in one or both spouses that manifest in negative behaviors, secrecy, and betrayal.

Let these stories be a cautionary tale for us all, because to the extent that we are unwilling to move beyond the money taboo, we all stand to carry a part of this shadow inside us. Every day, we hear news about some individual (or corporation — they have their own shadow aspects) who committed an act that no one saw coming or was, by all accounts, not in keeping with his or her core personality. This is always followed by statements like "But he was such a nice guy; what happened?" from those who knew the person. Our shadow aspects are generally hidden deep within us. Most of us work hard to overcome these tendencies, but we often discover the money shadow in others only when we get hit between the eyes.

In relationships, the money shadow can show up in a number of ways, but perhaps one of the most common is *financial infidelity*. According to a survey conducted by the National Endowment for Financial Education, over 58 percent of those surveyed reported that they hid money or purchases from their spouse. Over 34 percent indicated that they had previously lied to their spouse about their earnings, debt, or finances. What makes us do this? Our own unexplored money shadows. How can we change this? Let's start by getting out of the money closet, which is the first step to breaking free of the money taboo. We have everything to gain by doing this and increasingly more to lose if we continue to keep the deadbolt locked on the door. Can we really afford to lose any more? I don't think so. Today, with millions of people reaching their financial breaking point, the stakes are getting higher and the consequences are far greater than ever before. Financial planning will never be an adequate solution for the money issues that cause financial conflict, self-sabotage, and disharmony in relationships.

Humans have had a rather precarious relationship with money since it was first created. Historically, whenever we have lost our way with money, becoming increasingly greedy, overconsuming, and overindebted, we have experienced major economic challenges. Couples would be advised, as an ounce of prevention, to use this book as an opportunity to do some inner work and reflection. Given our individual and global economic challenges, this is not a good time in history to live in denial or, worse, arrogance. The spiritual and physical laws of the universe are such that great imbalances seldom are tolerated without consequence.

Whenever the doorway to any subject or issue is closed or off-limits, we remain trapped on the other side, without access to what might be possible, including solutions, understanding, and healing. Taboos are the breeding ground for fear, limitation, misunderstanding, and pain. Until we pry open the door and begin to explore the taboo subject of money, we remain imprisoned in systems that keep us stuck, fearful, and contracted. Once it's opened, we can begin to explore and discover new possibilities. We can learn new ways of being that are more expansive and allow us to feel safe enough to reflect and respond in healthier, more life-affirming ways.

In most families, when we are relatively young, money is established as a system of punishment and reward. This is where some of our money patterns and flawed beliefs take root. At the core of this is the gradual forming of an underlying belief that only *if* and *when* we are "good" are we worthy of receiving money. In sharp contrast, when we are "not good" or perhaps even told that we are "bad," we can develop the flawed belief that we must be unworthy of having or receiving money. I believe that people keep an unconscious tab of the things they've done wrong in their life that serve as evidence of why they have not experienced more money, success, or happiness. This unconscious checks-and-balances system is deeply flawed, simply because, as human beings, we are always *worthy*. If you are here, you were given the gift of life for a reason, and therefore you must be worthy of all life's possible expressions, including money.

When money (not unlike food, one of our other addictions) becomes a bargaining chip that parents use to get their children to behave and conform to *their* needs and desires, much can go wrong. This form of parenting can create a pattern of contradiction and confusion that is challenging for a child to understand and integrate. Another unpleasant side effect of this unconscious and seemingly benign form of manipulation is that those children may grow up to become adults who easily confuse their self-worth with their net worth. They may come to expect and believe that they get what they "deserve" or "do not deserve," which is a direct reflection of their value and self-esteem. Virginia Satir, one of the leading pioneers of family therapy, wrote, "Every word, facial expression, gesture, or action on the part of a parent gives the child some message about self-worth."

The person we grow into as an adult is largely shaped by what is referred to in money coaching as the *unconscious inheritance* — the money patterns of our family of origin, which are often fraught with conflict and contradictory behaviors.

We all need, require, and deserve food, shelter, love, and, yes, even money, to feel secure, grow, and thrive. These basic needs should never be given or withheld conditionally. When money (or food, shelter, or safety) is conditionally given to us or withdrawn, we can begin to believe that we are somehow not enough or are unworthy, which can damage our core self-esteem. It is critical to understand that while most parents don't intend to harm their children in this manner, unconscious parenting does often produce a harmful result. I see signs of this every day in my practice, and know too many adults who feel unworthy of having money or can have only just "enough" because their self-esteem will not allow them to imagine the possibility of more. This is the main reason why poverty is so deeply entrenched and difficult to overcome. Many people simply do not possess the container for a greater financial reality. Most people clearly want more money. Unfortunately, many do not possess the belief that they are worthy of it. This may explain why nine out of ten lottery winners spend or lose all their winnings within five years. For people with these unconscious money patterns, acquiring a great deal of money only serves to make matters worse.

By the time we reach adulthood, form relationships, and marry, our personal and financial self-esteem is already completely formed. Whatever modeling or messages we may have received have become hardwired patterns in the brain that are habitual and unconscious. We don't know much about this aspect of ourselves or our mates until we marry or live with each other and begin to share and experience money together. Imagine this scenario: You're a newlywed wife and have just spent a fortune on your wedding, the happiest day of your life. In fact, you've just returned from a marvelous honeymoon in Hawaii. The two of you couldn't be happier. A week later, the bills for your wedding and honeymoon arrive, and your dear husband hits the ceiling over unanticipated expenses. He becomes irate and blames *you* for not paying attention and overspending. He tells you, "I guess it's going to have to be me who handles the money from now on because you clearly are not capable! You're out to lunch when it comes to money! What do think — we're made of money?" You are startled and confused. You've never seen your man act like this! You feel ashamed and also angry. What is he so mad about? you wonder. It's only money, and we have more than enough! You feel very wounded and unsafe. From that day forward, you begin to hide your spending out of fear of your husband's anger and reactivity. And poof — there goes the intimacy! Both of you have become defensive, and now there is an invisible distance between you that grows larger with each secret purchase you make.

So what happened? With barely a blink, your husband unconsciously took on the role of his father ("I have to be the man and control the ship!"). And guess what? It's beginning to feel like the good old days, back at home with *your* father, the money tyrant who gave and withheld money and love based on whether or not you were good! Suddenly you have become the compliant wife on the outside and a rebellious teenager on the inside. Déjà vu? No, you both just became triggered by past wounds and unconsciously slipped into prescribed roles and money patterns with each other. The foundations of your patterns were laid long ago. They were silently and opportunistically waiting to meet up again in holy matrimony, where all of our deepest issues become triggered. Fortunately, there is help and hope for every couple willing to do the work.

Free Will and Money

Not only do we all need and deserve financial intimacy and security, but it is our birthright! We live in an abundant universe, and if we learn how to manage our resources more wisely, surely we should be able to find a way to properly support the basic needs of every human being on our planet. If this is true, why do so many feelings of fear and scarcity exist? The primary reason, in my observation, is that people live perpetually between two contradictory cycles: fear and greed. When the world feels safe and secure, we'll spend like there's no tomorrow, to the point of excess, greed, and overconsumption. The flip side of this occurs the minute our inner landscape gets triggered and we feel fearful or financially at risk. At this point, most people become emotional, impulsive, or reactive and begin to hold on to and protect whatever they have. People around the world experience this every day, even when there is no clear or present danger.

This cycle is emotional, not rational, and it is created by three overlapping factors: (1) the collective unconscious, in which the software program we came preloaded with has sectors that are infected by the money challenges brought down through the ages; (2) our hardwired brain patterning (caused by the phenomenon first identified by Donald Hebb, a Canadian neuropsychologist, and often paraphrased as "neurons that fire together, wire together"), which is formed in the brain during early childhood through our individual experiences; and (3) our basic biology, which automatically kicks in whenever we feel fearful or threatened. Remember studying about our prehistoric ancestors? Well, there's still a piece of them inside all of us, and it's called the *primitive brain*. We have not evolved beyond this dimension because we still need this part of the brain to get ourselves out of danger quickly when our safety is at risk. But we are prone to projection and often let our fears get the best of us. We tend to imagine the worst and worry without true cause, which only creates more fear and anxiety. Consequently, we tend to live our lives largely in fear of what might happen rather than experiencing what is actually happening, which is truly unfortunate.

The human brain is highly vulnerable to stress, and when we're worried about finances and money, it becomes flooded with cortisol, the stress hormone. Similar to when we flood the carburetor with too much gas, having too much cortisol in the brain can cause us to malfunction and reduces our ability to effectively problem solve or manage our financial challenges. In addition, too much stress can affect the level of serotonin (the well-being hormone) as well, which can lead to sadness, depression, and despair. Bottom line: money issues can impact the best of us. Whenever we become emotionally and financially imbalanced, our biochemistry is greatly impacted as well. So we need to become more knowledgeable about the relationship between money and the brain so that we may understand one another and live in greater harmony. The more conscious and aware of your inner dynamics, issues, and triggers you become, individually and as a couple, the greater your capacity to enhance your relationship. Over time, both of you can learn how to interrupt — or, more optimally, change — your money dynamics and thus improve your lives and financial outcomes.

Change Is a Choice

It is essential to remember the tremendous gift of free will that we were given at birth. No other species was given this gift! We must learn how to access the rich potentiality of our free will and to express it for the highest good of ourselves, our relationships, our community, and the planet. In doing so, we can become more powerful and empowering and will have greater access to fully receiving *all* of our good. This good is our divine inheritance, and it is already present and available to us all, though too few have learned how to access or utilize it properly. The exception to this, of course, occurs when our unconscious behaviors or shadow causes us to commit acts that are immoral, illegal, and harmful to others, causing us to literally lose access to free will and the world as punishment for the crime. Sometimes, however, we accidentally or inadvertently lose access to our own power and will as a result of accumulated pain and experiences that have become calcified inside of us. When this happens, we surrender our power and may consciously or subconsciously believe that we are not worthy and do not deserve, setting forth a path of self-fulfilling prophecy that perpetuates this belief, which is itself a lie. In my practice as a money coach, I see this reality manifested in my clients' lives in some of the following ways:

"If I don't have money, I am worthless" (as in "worth less").
"I must have done something terribly wrong to deserve this."
"I don't have the money gene."
"Nothing I do is ever enough."
"I'm cursed when it comes to money."
"I'm not smart enough/good enough."

We become deeply patterned at an early age. Not unlike the computer I just bought, we each come into the world with a preloaded software package called the *collective unconscious*. This package consists of the vast collection and archive of our human experience from the beginning of time, which represents the operating system that runs in the background of our human consciousness. Think of it as the hard drive of human existence. When we are born into the world and begin to have our own personal experiences, they become hardwired in the brain (which itself functions like a computer and is, in fact, more powerful than any computer that has ever been built). Now, add to this the awareness that money patterns and behaviors are often deeply entrenched family patterns that are passed down unconsciously from one generation to the next. The money patterns, behaviors, and beliefs that we inherit from our parents — and their parents before them — can be challenging for a number of reasons:

- We have very little, if any, formal training or education about money or personal finance.
- Money is a core survival issue and, as such, can cause us to become easily fearful and triggered.
- Money remains an unsafe or taboo subject in many families.
- Most of our core money patterns and behaviors become hardwired in early childhood and remain locked inside of us without exploration, awareness, or understanding.
- We avoid or are fearful of bringing these issues to light because of our internalized fears, anxiety, and shame.
- We carry money wounds that, left unhealed, become our shadow.

Love, Money, and Relationship Patterns

I remember spending hours as a little girl, daydreaming about finding my very own Prince Charming. Then, as I got older and started to date, it became clear to me that this was not going to be such an easy task. From the beginning, I felt very uncomfortable when I'd go out on a date and the boy would pick up the check. I felt awkward and "less than." This was, of course, during the time when it was still expected that the guy would pay for everything on a date. I've always been fiercely independent and have worked and had my own money since I was eight. So this caused me much discomfort and confusion. Over the years, I have discussed this topic with many women and discovered that most felt similar discomfort with this arrangement. In fact, many women felt that they owed the man something as a result of this transaction. And as it turns out, some of the men thought so, too. Sometimes, the women reported, they actually got it! Many women succumb to the pressure to have sex due to feelings of obligation or guilt that the man spent money on them. This is not right, nor does it serve either party. On the other side of the spectrum, men were given the burden of financial responsibility early on (although this has changed in many families today) to be the breadwinner and provide for the family. But no one ever bothered to ask them whether they wanted this responsibility or if they were in agreement with this prescribed role, which is simply not fair to men, either.

I'm amazed that this system is still very much intact and that many women and men still operate this way, even after they're married. Why? Because when we marry, we unconsciously move into prescribed roles that closely mirror those in our family of origin, and our underlying patterns and behaviors around money begin to unravel through unexpressed expectations and unconscious agreements. Throughout this book, you will be guided to understand how your own money patterns and behaviors influence your relationship with money as well as those of your spouse or partner. I refer to this in money coaching as "yours, mine, and ours" patterns because both partners enter the marriage with fairly established patterns, and then, over time, the couple develops its own distinct patterns ("ours"), which are often reactive and ineffective ways of being.

Our Money Issues as Symptoms

Money is a powerful energy force and medium of exchange. It is a tool and resource that we receive as a result of the actions and contributions we put forth in the world. It flows in and out of our lives in direct relationship to our efforts and intentions. Whenever you feel fearful or anxious about money, it is wise to spend some time in meditation or prayer to determine what inside of you might need attending to and to begin to address those needs proactively.

EXERCISE
Inner Resourcing

Spend five minutes reflecting on how you feel about money at this very moment. Questions to reflect and write about in your money coaching journal:

1. If money were your lover, how would describe your relationship with it? Estranged, detached, irritable, thoughtful, loving? Write about your feelings.
2. How do you feel about yourself and your relationship with money?
3. How do you feel about your partner and money? Write words that describe how you experience your partner with regard to money.

Couples generally come to see me because they believe that they have issues with money, which, on the surface anyway, may be the case. More often than not, however, their money issues are merely a *symptom* of another problem. For example, I have a client who is very talented and makes a good living in his business, but who worries incessantly about money. He thinks he has money issues, but the truth is, he has enough money and makes a good living. His real problems are (1) he hates what he does for a living and feels trapped and afraid of making a career change; (2) he lacks the confidence and faith that he can choose to do something else; and (3) he doesn't believe that he deserves to have what he wants, which is the heart of his problem.

Unfortunately, we often mistakenly believe that having more money is the cure to fixing or changing whatever isn't working in our life. Our tendency to focus on money as the problem and/or solution is really only a clever distraction from looking at the *real* problem. Beyond letting us meet our basic needs of food, shelter, and safety, money is seldom the answer to our life's problems and circumstances. Although having more money might help initially, if we haven't solved the underlying issues, then simply having more money often makes matters worse. We don't need to look very far to see evidence of wealthy people who have very big money issues.

In challenging financial times, I think it's important to focus not on the lack of money flowing into our lives but rather on what inside of us needs tending to and healing. As we are willing to step up and address what's really wrong, both in our economy and in our own personal finances, we can begin to solve the *real problems*. This book provides a road map for identifying and healing your relationship with money, individually and as a couple. Money coaching is a step-by-step process that can help you to discover how you are hardwired around money in ways that you may not be fully aware of. We all have money patterns and behaviors that create stress, anxiety, and fear, and that are contradictory to creating the personal and financial life we desire. If we don't know what these patterns are, how can we possibly change them? The money coaching processes used in this book will help you to do the following:

- Discover your *money types* and understand the impact they have on your life, your relationship, and your finances. (There are eight different money types, which will be explored further in chapter 3. You can also take the Money Type Quiz on my website, www.MoneyCoaching Institute.com.)

- Understand how your money patterns were formed in your family of origin and what you can do to change them.
- Remove unconscious obstacles or blocks that may be limiting your financial potential.
- Learn how to communicate and work more effectively with your spouse and family members around money issues.
- Learn new tools and strategies to change how you think, feel, and act with regard to money and personal finances.
- Develop new awareness, self-understanding, and peace of mind through creating a balanced life together — personally and financially.

Meaningful and sustainable change of any kind can take place only under certain conditions. In money coaching, we identify these conditions as follows:

1. Developing an understanding and new level of awareness of our core money patterns
2. The willingness to change, which involves doing something new and different from what we've been doing
3. Implementing new tools and behavior strategies
4. Accountability and action to create meaningful and lasting change

Remember, we were not given the proper training and education we needed to be financially successful, which often means that we have some *unlearning* to do before we can create and implement the new learning. Through our inner work and perseverance, we can begin to heal the money wounds that have caused us to become confused about what really matters. Money is a tool and powerful resource, but it is not something to make your life about, nor is it ever going to keep you warm at night or comfort you when you feel sad or lonely. Money cannot buy you anything that you *really* need outside of food and shelter. We forget that those who came before us lived for millions of years with little else and seem to have managed (albeit not as comfortably!).

Our money issues can, however, cause us to become confused about what really matters. They can lead us to believe that we need more than we do; make us desire things over people and our planet; and at times, when we are fearful, cause us to forget that, in the end, the only thing that can heal us or save us is love. As we begin to heal our lives and our relationships, we increase our capacity to create a far better, more financially mindful and sustainable world.

Chapter Two

YOUR MONEY STORY AND PERSONAL MYTHOLOGY

*The experiences and illuminations of childhood and early youth
become in later life the types, standards and patterns
of all subsequent knowledge and experience.*

— ARTHUR SCHOPENHAUER, quoted in Joseph Campbell,
A Joseph Campbell Companion

We all have a money story that began in our early childhood and evolved through time into our adulthood. Our money stories evolve out of our experience, through twists and turns, plots and subplots, and ultimately develop into the "story of our story" — our own personal mythology. Our individual mythologies are the narrative we use in daily life to express and explain how we came to be who we are. Our money stories and personal mythologies serve as a kind of guide and road map in helping us to navigate, discover, and create meaning out of our inner landscape, our experiences, and our lives.

My Early Money Story

When I was five years old, my "rich" aunt and uncle came to visit us and gave each of us children a crisp, new ten-dollar bill and said we could do anything we wanted with it. They took my sisters to the toy store, but I declined. I needed time to think about what I wanted to do with my money. Later that day, I walked to the corner store and asked the cashier for ten one-dollar bills. Then I went back to my neighborhood and gave nine of my one-dollar bills away to my friends, keeping one dollar for myself. It made me very happy to do this. Later that day, my mom came home and asked where my money was. I joyfully told her that I had given all but one dollar away to other kids on the block. She became angry and punished me for being "ungrateful" and for wasting what I had been given. She seemed embarrassed and ashamed of me. I felt sad and confused. If it felt good to give, how could it be bad? Wasn't it my money to do what I wanted with? "No" she said, "go get it back." Forced to ask for the money back, I felt deeply ashamed and humiliated.

I always knew we were poor, but by the age of eight, I began to realize that if I wanted anything, I'd have to learn how to get it on my own. So, I began my first entrepreneurial venture and ironed clothes for others, charging five cents per item. Later, I moved on to cleaning the houses of some of my mother's friends. I was good at cleaning and felt well paid, even though sometimes my arms hurt for days from washing windows. The ladies were kind to me and fixed me sandwiches for lunch. I didn't mind that other kids played while I worked. I had my own money and used or saved it as I pleased. Mostly, I liked to save it for something special.

My mother worked long hours as a waitress. I remember feeling sad that she had to work so hard. Most of my friends' mothers stayed at home and didn't have to work. This didn't seem fair to me. I tried to keep the house clean to make my mom happy.

I was an exceptional student and almost always got straight As. Sometimes I would be given a dollar for each A, but only for the As. I soon learned that Bs or below were "worthless," and this made me feel confused and angry. Why are Bs not good enough? I thought. They should be worth at least fifty cents if an A is worth a dollar.

Every September, my mother took us shopping for school clothes. We always shopped at sales, but sometimes Mom would treat us and let us shop at Robinson's (a chic and more expensive store), which is where she said the rich people shopped. She was the queen of bargain hunting. Before we got home, Mom would make us put our "loot" into Kmart shopping bags and hide the evidence of the Robinson's bags in the trash. We were sworn to secrecy. Mom always said, "We may be poor, but you'll always look rich." How we looked was very important to her. We didn't have much, and what we bought was always on sale, but it was always nice. I felt this was the way we hid our poverty, as though it was something to be ashamed of.

My father gave his paycheck to Mom every week, and she handled the finances. I somehow knew that there was never enough and that she struggled to make do with what there was. We ate a lot of beans and potatoes. Sometimes, when things were really tight, my mom would make a chocolate cake, and we'd eat chocolate cake with beans on top. This was our family's version of a gourmet meal. It helped to compensate for another night of beans and felt like a celebration to us.

When I was ten, my father lost his blue-collar job at the steel factory where he was a foreman. They closed the plant due to the recession (the oil crisis of the early seventies). He could not find work, so we moved from California to Utah, where he was offered a job. We were very sad in Utah and were treated like foreigners. One day, I woke up and found my mom packing up our things. She said that we were moving that week to Arkansas. We were shocked. Mom was frantic and said that something bad was going to happen if we didn't leave. She had had a premonition. We packed and left like gypsies in the night. Our two brothers promised to move and join us later. I felt very scared. We had little money, and my dad had no job.

We drove nonstop to my grandparents' house in Batesville, Arkansas. They were dirt-poor and lived in the boonies. But there was no work, no money, and no future in Arkansas, and soon we left. We drove to St. Louis to see if my dad could find a job there. We moved in with my aunt, who was a widow and lived alone in the ghetto, but she refused to move. There I briefly found a home as one of the only white kids in a poor African American neighborhood that filled my life with a sense of belonging. Being poor didn't matter. I was accepted and even allowed to perform as one of the "Supremes" (in my Afro wig!) in our makeshift neighborhood street theater. I felt rich for the first time.

When I was twelve, we moved into our own house, which was in a horribly poor neighborhood. Within a few months, I awoke early one morning to hear my mother screaming and crying. I walked into the kitchen and discovered that our older brother had been killed in a hunting accident in Utah. Something bad had happened there; Mom's premonition came true. My brother's death devastated our family. We barely had enough money to get to California to bury our brother in the family cemetery. When we returned home, we didn't have enough money to rent our own place. My parents asked their best friends if we could stay with them until we got on our feet, but they said no. This crushed my mother's spirit. She had just lost her son and had traveled all that way to bury him, and her friends couldn't find it in their hearts to help us. Our dog even died on the way home from heat exposure. My parents never bad-mouthed those friends. They said they understood, but it took me years to forgive this betrayal. Everything else during this time is a blur, except that my mother was devastated, and we didn't have enough money to bury our brother properly. I don't think my family ever recovered.

We moved into a housing project and were forced to go on welfare. The recession continued, and my father still could not find work. Living in the projects was a trip. I quickly made friends in my now very racially mixed neighborhood and attempted to make the most of it. I focused on and excelled in school and was named student of the year. I wanted to compensate for my mother's loss by doing well. I kept myself so busy that I didn't have time to feel poor, until one day I was chased by giant cockroaches in our apartment.

The next year, my father finally found work, and we moved to a better neighborhood. Now fourteen, I began working at Taco Bell. I loved making my own money and not having to ask anyone for *anything*. Fiercely independent, I had one and sometimes two jobs from that age on. Work had become my refuge from a difficult life. Working and making money were my ticket out of that life.

I saved enough money to buy my own car at sixteen. I surprised my parents one day when I drove into the driveway with my primer-gray Buick LeSabre. They were stupefied and couldn't understand how I kept figuring out all this money stuff on my own. They wouldn't let me have a driver's license, but I had bought my own car!

I decided to go to college, and with the help of my high school counselor, I received scholarships and grants. When I told my parents that I'd been accepted to a top university, they laughed and said, "Yeah, right... who's going to pay for that?" I told them, "Don't worry, I've already figured it all out, and you won't need to pay a dime." That night, my father came into my room and told me that he was very proud of me and of what I had accomplished. It was the first time he had ever truly acknowledged me. Shortly after that evening, on the night of my high school graduation, my father died suddenly from a massive heart attack. He never made it to my graduation. He was only fifty, and his life had ended, all too abruptly.

With his passing, my mother became a young widow and single parent of three. All that my father left her was a $10,000 life insurance policy, which my financially naive mother thought was a small fortune. Within a year, she began to realize that $10,000 would not last us very long. Now, with only a waitress's income, my mother simply couldn't make ends meet, and money was a source of constant stress and struggle from then on. She never really recovered emotionally or financially from my father's death. When she died, she had very little to speak of materially, which bothered her greatly. But she was a great mother who did the best she could with what she had.

I became the first and only person in my family to attend and graduate from college. Having witnessed so much financial struggle in my parents' lives has deeply influenced my own life and choices. It is part of my own personal mythology and has informed my destiny. I was determined to learn how to be financially educated and empowered, and to help others to do so, too.

Understanding Our Stories

Each of our stories is rich with meaning and metaphor. We are not unlike great stone carvings being shaped into human form by our trials and tribulations. When we merge into relationship, our individual stories also merge and become entwined. The problem is, when it comes to money, our partners seldom fully know or comprehend the significance of these stories in our de-velopment. Without our stories, we cannot make sense of how our money patterns and behaviors were formed. Knowing each other's money stories is essential to understanding present-day money patterns and behaviors. Without this understanding, we are prone to making assumptions, drawing conclusions, and, worse, judging one another. The sharing of our stories not only helps us to make sense of our own experience but also helps our partners to do the same.

EXERCISE

Writing Your Money Story

I strongly encourage you both to write and share your individual money stories with each other. I recommend that you use this process as the foundation and building blocks of creating financial intimacy, which will deepen your relationship.

STEP ONE. WRITE YOUR STORY: Begin by writing your money story from childhood to the point where you first met your partner. Write your story from your earliest money memory, and move chronologically through time, allowing your memories to come in one at a time. It is best to write your money story in a stream-of-consciousness manner without editing, judging, or analyzing your memories while writing. Include as much detail as you can, as it will help you to identify your money patterns and relevant themes. When you reach the point in your life where you met your current partner or spouse, title the next section "The Story of Us," and write your money memories from when you began dating to your present-day life together.

STEP TWO. MAP YOUR STORY: Once you've completed your story, read it from the beginning to identify recurring patterns, themes, emotions, and beliefs. Below is an example of one client's story map. On a separate sheet of paper or in your money journal, map your story, using this example as a template.

EXAMPLE: *Story Mapping*	
Money Patterns	**Money Themes**
Giving	Feast or famine
Confused	Never enough
Need my own money	Loss and betrayal
Work hard	Survivor
Sacrifice	Scarcity
Creative	Rich versus poor
Resourceful	Hide poverty
Fiercely independent	Work = money + independence
Money Emotions	**Money Beliefs**
Happy	Money is hard to get/keep.
Joyful	There will never be enough.
Sadness	Money is not fair.
Worried	Money is stressful.
Fear	Rich people are selfish.
Anger	Money is not for our family.
Resentment	To be poor is shameful.
Humiliated	Making money is hard work.

EXERCISE
Money Messages and Meaning

Before you proceed, take some time to reflect on these questions and write in your journal.

1. What messages about money did you receive in your childhood from your parents?
2. How do those messages influence and inform your experience with money today?
3. What would you have rather heard or experienced that might have made a difference?
4. How have your money patterns changed since childhood?
5. What messages about money are you giving or would you like to give to your partner or children, if you have them?
6. If money were not an obstacle, real or perceived, what would you do differently in your life today?

Sharing Your Money Story

Now that you've written your money story, it is time to share it. Before you do, I suggest that you make an agreement with your partner to listen to each other's stories from a place of nonjudgment and compassion. Ask your partner for this agreement in advance. Once you've agreed, take turns reading your stories aloud without interruption. Once you've both read your stories, discuss them openly. Here are some questions to help guide your discussion:

1. What did you learn about me that was new?
2. What was uncomfortable for you to share and why?
3. What fears or emotions came up as you were sharing?
4. What surprised you most about my story?
5. What helped you to understand me and my money patterns more?
6. Was there anything about my story that was confusing or that you would like to know more about?

"The Story of Us"

Now that you've read and discussed your individual "Story of Us" memories, notice what you both chose to write about and any significant differences in perspectives. For example, do you have similar or different recollections about how you navigated through money issues in your relationship? If so, please know that this is not uncommon. Most of us tend to remember things in relationship to our own experience rather than our partner's. However, noticing how your partner's perspective is different from your own can be enlightening, providing new awareness and perspective, and can even help you to know what to do differently in the future.

For example, when I read the money stories of my clients John and Ann, I noticed that their memories about an early financial agreement were radically different. It was apparent that they'd been operating from assumptions rather than facts. Before they married, John believed that he had been clear about not wanting to be financially responsible for Ann and about the fact that he expected her to pay for her own expenses as well as contribute to their joint expenses. Ann, on the other hand, said that her husband did not want to be responsible for her personal expenses *only*. Over the years, she had pretty much covered her own personal expenses, such as her car payment, credit card payment, hair and beauty costs, clothes, and groceries. She had "let" John, who earned considerably more, cover the larger expenses, such as their mortgage, taxes, insurance, and vacations. John's money story indicated that he felt resentful about this.

As we discussed their situation, they began to see how this pattern had evolved out of a miscommunication. In fact, Ann was happy to pay more to help support their household but had received mixed messages from John. He liked being in charge of their financial house and being the primary breadwinner. However, he sometimes felt taken advantage of — that he was carrying the bulk of the financial burden. He was conflicted and therefore gave mixed messages to Ann. Through their stories, they were able to see where the communication had gone awry, and they were able to work together to resolve it amicably.

As you learn more about each other through this storytelling process, it is important to determine if there are any communication or money issues to discuss and resolve before moving forward.

Writing Your Next Chapter

Regardless of your history, which cannot be undone, the future is still unwritten and can be altered by your present-day awareness and intentions moving forward. How would you both like to have your money story unfold from here? Start the next chapter of your story together based on what you would like to create.

What old money patterns would you each like to overcome?
What new money patterns would you each like to develop?
What money themes would you like to change or embrace?

What new emotions would you like to experience?
What beliefs about money would you like to surrender?
What new money beliefs would you like to develop?
What is the vision you hold for your future together, personally and financially?

Write all this down and begin to co-create it today.

Chapter Three

YOURS, MINE, AND OURS: MONEY PATTERNS

To understand is to perceive patterns.

— Isaiah Berlin, *The Proper Study of Mankind*

We are all looking for a home for our heart, our very own safe harbor from the often-stormy sea of life. When we find our love, we experience great joy, gratitude, and contentment unlike anything we have previously known. For a while, we feel that we have finally arrived and nuzzle up to our daily lives together filled with moments of closeness and happiness. As our fantasy slowly drifts into reality, with schedules, routines, and the complications that life often brings without warning or reprieve, we begin to realize that relationships are often more hard work than bliss. Of course, this does not mean that we no longer love our lives and our partners, but as the newness and shine wear off, we are left to live with what our relationship really is, rather than our fantasy. When we become aware that our fantasy has been replaced by reality, we find ourselves at a crossroads in our relationship.

This phase of relationship is the perfect time to examine our individual and relationship patterns and commit to the long haul. Failure to do this often results in the development of unconscious compensation systems that can erode the intimacy in our relationships. This may manifest as an increased demand for something external, say a new car or home, to replace our unmet emotional needs. Left unmanaged, this behavior can develop into unhealthy money patterns, in which couples project their unresolved issues, silent expectations, and demands onto their partners. As healthy, mature adults, we must seize this time as an opportunity to create something deeper and more meaningful, which hopefully is why you are reading this book.

Millions of couples experience feelings of disappointment in the marriage or partnership around money and their financial circumstances, among other things. The problem began, however, not in the later stages of your relationship but rather in the beginning, with patterns that most likely developed prior to the relationship. Nor can our relationships solve what is unresolved within us. The very idea that someone else can somehow magically complete us is deeply flawed. This romantic notion that human beings have held on to for centuries, implying that we are broken or somehow incomplete without our other half, is absurd.

The greatest and most worthy use of our life's energy is the pursuit of knowing, loving, and accepting ourselves and each other as Spirit does, fully and unconditionally. When we can do this, we can love others fully and unconditionally without projecting our needs and expectations onto them to somehow "fix" us as evidence and proof of their love and thus prove that we are worthy of love. Couples' lives can unintentionally become expressions of their inner discontent and disconnectedness from themselves and each other.

One way this manifests is in "keeping up with the Joneses" with the insatiable pursuit of more and better. Ironically, this cycle, known as the *hedonic treadmill*, has been studied and proven to be merely the beginning of the end, because the minute we step onto that treadmill, we have lost. We have entered a game that we cannot win because we can never keep up. There will always be someone with more, bigger, and better. True happiness and contentment is the by-product not of having more but rather of feeling content and grateful with what you do have. Contentment is not a club you can buy your way into but one you earn your way into through the deep and relentless pursuit of self-awareness, healing, and spiritual work. The only reason why anyone would feel the need to "keep up with the Joneses" would be because they felt somehow incomplete and insufficient as they were.

We may falsely believe that if we can't have what we really want and desire, and even the love of our life has failed to complete us, then maybe we can buy a better life with more, bigger, and better stuff. We fool ourselves into believing that somehow we'll find the magic key out there, when all along, it was inside of us. But the key to happiness is not out there; it is in here, inside us, and no one or no material thing can ever give that to us. It's not theirs to give. It cannot be given to us, but we can learn how to receive it.

My husband was a bachelor until he was fifty. He'd had several relationships but never married. When we met and then married a few years later, I asked him what had changed for him and why he decided that he wanted to marry after all those years. His response was interesting and humbling: "For the first time, I felt I was with someone who didn't expect me to be the one to fix her or make her life okay. I didn't want that job or to become the person who somehow disappointed them. You were different. You know who you are and take responsibility for your own happiness." It's not your spouse's job to make you happy. It's your job. On the other hand, if you're with someone who is selfish, unloving, or unkind, it may be difficult to be happy with a person such as this in your life.

However, we are free to choose the life we inhabit. As free human beings, we have the right to choose to live differently if the life we are in does not support our highest good. We can also choose, today, to change the relationship we are currently in by realizing that we have projected all of our unmet needs and expectations unrealistically onto our partner and, in doing so, set ourselves up for disappointment and hurt.

Money Types and Your Relationship

At the Money Coaching Institute, we help people to identify and understand their money patterns and behaviors by working with their *money types*. Money types are archetypes that serve as shorthand to understanding our behaviors, and they exist inside of all of us. They are not just more labels meant to define us; rather, they are a powerful way of helping us to gain awareness about our relationship to money. Your money types are not your personality or who *you are* at all. However, your money types can help you to understand *where you are* with regard to money and your financial life — and perhaps even help you to know how you got there.

My previous book *Money Magic: Unleashing Your True Potential for Prosperity and Fulfillment* describes eight money types that encompass our collective money patterns and behaviors.

Recognizing these types will help you to work together as a couple to improve your financial life.

The Eight Money Types

Most people fit one or more of the eight money types. Different from true Jungian archetypes, which define various personality types, your money types are, again, *not* your personality, nor are they in any way fixed. Rather, this system offers a simple way to identify and understand your patterns and behaviors relative to money. With this new understanding, you can change your money types, learn how to make more conscious choices, and, as a result, improve the money dynamics in your relationship.

I often refer to the eight money types as the characters that live inside of our everyday money drama (or comedy, as the case may be!). We might be successful in most areas of our lives, but when faced with money decisions, changes, or crises, many of us revert to an ineffective, emotional approach to making decisions about money. By understanding your unconscious patterns and beliefs about money, both you and your partner can become more conscious and aware. Over time, you will learn how to change your habitual money behaviors by noticing them when they show up, as they do daily. The following are descriptions of the eight money types.

The Innocent

The Innocent takes the ostrich approach to money matters. Innocents often live in denial, burying their heads in the sand where money is concerned. Since Innocents are easily overwhelmed by financial information, they usually rely heavily on the advice and opinions of others. Innocents are perhaps the most trusting of all the money types because they so greatly want to be rescued and taken care of that they do not see others for who they truly are. Innocents are childlike in the sense that they have not yet learned how to judge or discern other people's motives and behavior. While this trait can be endearing, it is also precarious for an adult trying to cope in the real world. We all start out our journey in life as Innocents; however, as we grow and develop, most of us shed the veil of innocence and replace it with discernment gained through experience. The Innocent's goal is safety at all costs, and they often have a fear of abandonment.

CHARACTERISTICS OF THE INNOCENT TYPE

- Trusting
- Indecisive
- Happy-go-lucky (externally)
- Fearful or anxious (internally)
- Financially dependent
- Nonconfrontational
- Feels powerless
- Represses feelings and beliefs
- Seeks security

The Victim

The Victim money type tends to live in the past and blame his or her financial woes on external factors. Passive-aggressive (prone to expressing their feelings in indirect rather than direct ways) in nature, Victims may appear outwardly as Innocents, because they seem so powerless and want others to take care of them. However, this appearance is often an unconscious pattern developed to get others to do for them what they refuse to do for themselves.

Victims generally have a litany of excuses for why they are not more financially successful, which are based on their historical mythology. That is not to say that bad things haven't happened to Victims. More often than not, Victims have been abused or betrayed or have suffered some great loss. The problem is that they have never processed their pain, acknowledged their part, or taken responsibility for the present. Victims are always looking for someone to rescue them, because they feel an underlying sense of entitlement as compensation for their suffering.

CHARACTERISTICS OF THE VICTIM TYPE

- Prone to blaming others
- Highly emotional (melancholy or angry)
- Lives in the past
- Financially irresponsible
- Seeks to be rescued
- Resentful
- Unforgiving
- Addictive
- Lives out a self-fulfilling prophecy
- Feels powerless

For the Victim's paradigm to shift, he or she must learn how to understand and heal past wounds. Of all the money types I have worked with, Victims are the most resistant to change. As a result, they stay stuck in their financial dramas, which are little more than reruns of the past.

The Warrior

The Warrior sets out to conquer the money world and is generally seen as successful in the business and financial worlds. Warriors are adept investors — focused, decisive, and in control. Although Warriors will listen to advisers, they make their own decisions and rely on their own instincts and resources to guide them. The world is filled with Warrior types, from those who are fierce allies and collaborators to those for whom making money is a form of competition and sport.

CHARACTERISTICS OF THE WARRIOR TYPE

- Powerful
- Driven
- Loyal
- Competitive
- Disciplined
- Goal-oriented
- Financially successful
- Confident
- Calculating
- Generous
- Rescuer
- Wise
- Discerning

The primary fears of the Warrior are dependence and loss of power. We all need a healthy Warrior inside of us. The Warrior is the archetype of action and is generally the archetype we want to call on to make things happen in our career and financial life. The Warrior aspect within us never gives up and is not easily defeated.

The Martyr

Martyrs are so busy taking care of others' needs that they often neglect their own. Financially speaking, Martyrs generally do more for others than they do for themselves. They often rescue others (such as a child, spouse, friend, or relative) from their financial circumstances or life crises. However, Martyrs' gifts may have strings attached, and if so, they may repeatedly feel let down when others fail to meet their expectations. The strongest indicator of the Martyr is self-sacrifice and an unconscious attachment to his or her suffering.

CHARACTERISTICS OF THE MARTYR TYPE

- Controlling
- Feels unappreciated
- Long-suffering
- Difficulty receiving
- Caretaker
- Self-sacrificing
- Disappointed
- Rescuer
- Perfectionist
- Resentful
- Passive-aggressive
- Compassionate
- Wise

Martyrs tend to be perfectionists and have high expectations of themselves and others, which makes them quite capable of realizing their dreams because they put so much energy into being right. Martyrs who are willing to do their own spiritual work to heal their wounds have the capacity to become gifted healers and powerful manifestors.

The Fool

The Fool plays by a different set of rules altogether. A gambler by nature, the Fool is always looking for a windfall by taking financial shortcuts. Even though the adage "A fool and his money are soon parted" may have some truth, Fools often win because they are willing to throw the dice; they are willing to take chances. An adventurer at heart, the Fool gets caught up in the enthusiasm of the moment, caring little for the details. Fools are relatively fearless in their endeavors and remain eternal optimists regardless of the circumstances. In this regard, Fools are like Warriors because they always seem to land on their feet and are not easily defeated. The Fool is much more interested in making money as a sport or form of recreation than as a serious endeavor.

The Fool does possess some rather remarkable qualities that, if mastered, make him or her quite capable of becoming a money Magician. The Fool lives very much in the moment and is quite unattached to future outcomes. A Fool pursues mostly for the simple pleasure of the pursuit. Many of us could learn from this characteristic of the Fool. However, until Fools become enlightened, they will continue to attract money easily, only to have it quickly slip through their fingers because they are simply not paying attention.

CHARACTERISTICS OF THE FOOL TYPE

- Restless
- Undisciplined

- Financially irresponsible
- Impetuous
- Optimistic
- Overly generous
- Happy-go-lucky
- Adventurous
- Lives for today

The Creator/Artist

Creator/Artists are on a spiritual, creative, or artistic path. They often find living in the material world difficult and frequently have a conflicted love/hate relationship with money. They love money for the freedom it buys them but would prefer not to have to sell themselves or their gifts in order to make a living. The Creator/Artist often overly identifies with the interior world and may even resent or despise those who are wealthy. Their negative beliefs about money and materialism only block them from the very freedom they so desire. Creator/Artists most fear being inauthentic or not being true to themselves.

Creator/Artists are the most conflicted about money of all the archetypes, which can sabotage their ability to manifest it. Too many people on the creative/artistic path feel that money is bad or lacking in spirituality. To the extent that Creator/Artists maintain this belief system, they are limiting themselves and creating a block to the flow of money.

The Creator/Artists who work to integrate the spiritual with the material world will find a solution to their financial struggles. Since they have spent much of their time and attention on their inner journey and creative potential, Creator/Artists already possess many of the qualities necessary to become money Magicians. This money type most needs to accept the outer world and embrace its many dimensions. To stop suffering from the tension they feel between the spiritual and material worlds, they must learn to embrace both worlds as part of their own duality.

CHARACTERISTICS OF THE CREATOR/ARTIST TYPE

- Highly artistic and/or spiritual
- Passive
- Internally motivated
- Detached
- Nonmaterialistic
- Visionary
- Truth seeker

The Tyrant

Tyrants use money to control people, events, and circumstances. The Tyrant hoards money, using it to manipulate and control others. Although Tyrants may have everything they need or desire, they never feel complete, comfortable, or at peace. The Tyrant's greatest fear is loss of control. Tyrants are often overdeveloped Warriors who have become highly invested in their need for control and dominance. While Warriors are often heroic in their true concern for others' welfare, Tyrants are purely self-interested. This money type wants power and control for their own sake and will forsake other people if necessary to gain more of it.

Throughout history, the Tyrant has emerged as the ruler who dominates and destroys with no sign of remorse. Today, Tyrants can be found among the political leaders, businesspeople, and family figureheads who use whatever means necessary to win. The Tyrant is a master manipulator of both people and money. Perhaps it's because the Tyrant type is presented as the image of financial success in our society that so many of us secretly believe money is bad. Television and the media do their part to further convince us that although we may think we want more money, we fear losing ourselves and becoming caught up in the greed and pursuit of power — like the Tyrant.

Tyrants, however, are not as rich as they appear. Sure, they have everything money can buy (which often includes beautiful people) and never have to worry about paying the phone bill, but they lack many things that money *cannot* buy. They are often, in spite of their apparent success, very fearful and rarely feel any sense of fulfillment. The Tyrant suffers from a condition I call "chronic-not-enoughness."

CHARACTERISTICS OF THE TYRANT

- Controlling
- Fearful
- Manipulative
- Oppressive
- Prone to anger
- Critical and judgmental
- Aggressive
- Unforgiving
- Secretive
- Highly materialistic

The Magician

The Magician is the ideal money type. Using a new and ever-changing set of dynamics in both the material and spirit worlds, Magicians know how to transform and manifest their own financial reality. At our best, when we are willing to claim our own power, we are all Magicians.

Magicians are fully awake and aware of themselves and the

world around them. They are armed with knowledge of the past, have made peace with their personal history, and understand that their power exists in their ability to see and live the truth of who they are. Magicians know that their ability to manifest lies with their Higher Power. With faith, love, and patience, the Magician simply waits in certainty with the knowledge that all our needs are met all the time. Magicians embrace the inner life as the place of spiritual wealth and the outer life as the expression of enlightenment in the material world.

CHARACTERISTICS OF THE MAGICIAN TYPE

- Spiritual
- Wise
- Conscious
- Unattached
- Trusting
- Generous
- Loving
- Fluid
- Lives in the present
- Powerful
- Optimistic
- Confident
- Compassionate
- Open to flow
- Financially balanced

Becoming a Magician is not just about having more money. It is a journey of discovery and exploration of your relationship with money and how that relationship helps you with, or distracts you from, living your life purpose and experiencing your full potential. Depending on your life's path and purpose, that may or may not be about becoming a millionaire. If you are attached to having great wealth as your outcome, you may be disappointed. I don't subscribe to pseudospiritual philosophies that promote quick fixes to bring instant wealth without any personal effort or commitment. All meaningful and sustainable change is a process that takes time. But don't let that discourage you or your partner, as this process is worth every minute and effort because it will change your life and your relationship as well.

What would your relationship be like if you and your partner were money Magicians? You could certainly anticipate that your stresses and fears around money would be greatly alleviated. You might also be more prosperous, or at least certainly able to enjoy the money you have together with greater joy. Money coaching will help you to align at both the inner and outer levels. You will learn more about money itself, and you may find yourself becoming more organized and developing better financial plans.

Using this coaching process as a tool in your relationship has another benefit that may not be apparent but is as valuable as all the material or monetary gains that you could ever achieve. This coaching process engages you and your partner to discover key issues that could become toxic in your relationship and family if never resolved. In relationships, money Magicians transform themselves by realizing that in the end, their life's journey was never about the money — it was about safety, trust, love, self-worth, honesty, appreciation, faith, compassion, and purpose. These are powerful gifts to bring to your relationship, and I wish them for both you and your partner.

Acknowledging the archetypes that are active in your lives is a starting point for transforming your relationship. By understanding each other's money history and the mythology associated with your current money types, you will become conscious of the patterns and behaviors that are preventing you from being strong Warrior-Magicians, the most powerful combination of the archetypes.

Money Type Quiz

Circle all the characteristics that apply to you regarding your tendencies around money.

1	Anxious		2	Prone to blame
3 & 7	Financially successful		2 & 5	Financially irresponsible
2	Lives in the past		1 & 2	Feels powerless
1	Financially dependent		2	Self-fulfilling prophecy
1 & 8	Trusting		3	Disciplined
2	Addictive		8	Confident
1	Naïve		4	Difficulty receiving
4	Feels betrayed		5	Careless
7	Judgmental		8	Conscious
3 & 4	Rescuer		1 & 5	Happy-go-lucky
3 & 8	Resourceful		2 & 4	Long-suffering
4 & 7	Manipulative		2 & 4	Passive-aggressive
4 & 7	Controlling		3 & 8	Wise
4	Self-sacrificing		5 & 8	Optimistic
4 & 8	Compassionate		6 & 8	Authentic
5	Undisciplined		7	Materialistic

5	Impulsive	6 & 8	Visionary
5	Adventurous	8	Unattached
6	Detached	7	Obsessive
6	Internally motivated	4	Unsupported
8	Balanced	5	Reckless
6	Passive	7	Angry
1 & 6	Nonconfrontational	6	Resistant
6 & 8	Creative	1, 2 & 7	Fearful
8	Transforms reality	5	Overly generous
6 & 8	Spiritual	8	Successful
7	Oppressive	6	Reclusive
4	Perfectionist	6	Nonmaterialistic
2	Highly emotional	1	Indecisive
1	Seeks rescue	1	Seeks security
2 & 7	Unforgiving	7	Secretive
3 & 8	Powerful	3	Collaborative
3	Goal-oriented	5	Overindulgent
3 & 7	Calculating	5	Restless
5	Lives for today	3	Loyal
3 & 8	Generous	6	Conflicted
8	Guided by faith	3	Cautious
3	Discerning	1	Represses feelings and beliefs
4	Caretaker		
2	Resentful		

Each characteristic in the quiz has one to three numbers to its left. Each of these numbers corresponds to one of the eight money types. Below is a list of the money types with their corresponding numbers. Add up the total count you have circled for each number. If you have circled a characteristic with two or more numbers, count that characteristic for each money type to which it applies.

Money Type Count from Key	Example
1 = Innocent _____	III (3)
2 = Victim _____	II (2)
3 = Warrior _____	И́tI (6)
4 = Martyr _____	И́t (5)
5 = Fool _____	II (2)
6 = Creator/Artist _____	II (2)
7 = Tyrant _____	IIII (4)
8 = Magician _____	И́tIIII (8)

The category in which you have the highest number indicates your primary money type. A score of five or more in *any* category indicates your active money types. These are the types that actively rule your financial life and decisions. A score of four or less represents a passive money type. While passive money types are generally not present or active in your daily life, they can be triggered and become active during times of stress or when you feel anxious or fearful about money.

Identifying Your Money Shadows

A score of five or more in any category represents an active money type that is present in your life right now. If you are not consciously aware of these characteristics, it is generally because they embody hidden or shadow aspects of yourself that you have not been ready (or willing) to look at. However, since awareness is the beginning of transformation, this is an opportune time to examine and understand your *money shadow*. We all possess a shadow side that represents hidden, secret, or disowned parts of ourselves. These aspects are fragmented parts of the self that remain unclaimed and therefore disconnected from the whole. We learn at an early age to "put our best face forward" in order to get our needs met or avoid rejection. This is costly to the self because it causes us to feel that we are not seen, loved, or appreciated for all that we are. We feel that we must, in fact, hide parts of who we are.

Inherited Money Patterns

In addition to our individual money patterns and behaviors, we possess the unconscious legacy of our family of origin. While we are children growing up, we take in everything around us, like little sponges. When our parents are stressed about money or become emotional and reactive, it leaves a lasting impression and pattern within us as well. This is why it is so critical to watch our language and behaviors relative to money in the presence of our children.

Thomas and Julia's Familial Money Patterns

Below is an overview of the inherited money patterns that Thomas and Julia unconsciously acquired from their families of origin.

JULIA'S INHERITED MONEY PATTERNS — FROM MOTHER

Anxious
Worried

49

Self-sacrificing
Passive-aggressive
Compassionate
Financially successful
Fearful
Overly generous
Caretaker
Critical
Judgmental
Secretive
Never enough
Frugal
Worried
Responsible

JULIA'S INHERITED MONEY PATTERNS — FROM FATHER

Wise
Financially successful
Optimistic
Hardworking
Powerful
Confident
Generous
Loving
Secretive
Open
Confident
Strong-willed
Provider
"Everything always works out"

JULIA'S INDIVIDUATED MONEY PATTERNS (NOT INHERITED)

Disciplined
Seeks security
Conscious
Thoughtful
Faith
Spiritual
Flow

THOMAS'S INHERITED MONEY PATTERNS — FROM MOTHER

Caring
Tries hard
Insecure
Defensive
Uncertain

THOMAS'S INHERITED MONEY PATTERNS — FROM FATHER

Opinionated
Spends beyond means
Lives for today
Controlled by spouse
Lacking power

THOMAS'S INDIVIDUATED MONEY PATTERNS (NOT INHERITED)

Vital
Empowered

Thomas's and Julia's mother and father pattern lists indicate the money patterns and behaviors that they have inherited from their parents. These patterns became hardwired early in their lives even before either of them knew much about the world of money. When they married, the patterns highlighted became emotionally triggered. This happens in all of our relationships, and to the extent that we identify unhealthy patterns and work to resolve them, they can be healed.

Common Archetype Pairings in Couples

There are any number of possible pairings within this archetypal system. To determine your primary relationship archetypes, first take the Money Type Quiz and determine your individual money types. Once you have both determined your active, primary money types, it is fairly easy to ascertain the *money style* of your relationship. Below are descriptions of the *dominant, passive,* and *mixed* archetype pairings that are most commonly seen between partners. While some couples have two dominant archetypes, even more couples have a dominant/passive pairing, in which one partner tends to take more of the lead relative to money and personal finances.

The dominant archetypes — the Warrior, Martyr, Fool, and Tyrant — are generally more actively engaged in the money dynamics of a given relationship. The passive archetypes — the Innocent, Victim, and Creator/Artist — tend to be less engaged or may prefer not to engage in money matters at all if given the option. The Magician is the "ideal" money type and is a purely positive influence; this aspect does not create imbalances as the other types do, and therefore it is not included in the Passive/ Dominant pairings below.

Common Dominant Archetype Pairings

WARRIOR–WARRIOR. In this pairing, which is fairly uncommon in my experience, the two Warriors would most likely be viewed as a "power couple." This means they are both highly financially goal-oriented, are strong earners, and are great at making and growing their money. The only downside is that they may become competitive with each other or may both want to lead, which can cause friction and possible intimacy issues.

WARRIOR–MARTYR. This pairing can also be very powerful, but the Martyr may feel that it is their role to take care of others more (such as rescuing adult children), and the Warrior may tire of this. The Martyr is more likely to have boundary issues and may feel that it is okay to sacrifice oneself for the benefit of others. The Warrior partner can become resentful of this and may become emotionally distant and feel put upon by their Martyr partner.

WARRIOR–FOOL. Warriors do not suffer fools very well at all. In fact, a true Warrior archetype can easily begin to disrespect their Fool partner due to the partner's inability to see the big picture. In general, the Warrior has a low tolerance for anyone they see as undisciplined, impulsive, or unable to make wise financial decisions. There is tremendous room for conflict in this archetypal pairing.

WARRIOR–TYRANT. These two archetypes may butt heads a great deal, as they both can be competitive, and the Tyrant does not acquiesce to other people's needs easily. There are often power and control issues between these two, as neither is likely to surrender control and both may want to lead, making it hard to maintain intimacy.

MARTYR–MARTYR. Observing this couple is often like watching a marathon of complaints, as both parties tend to be major caretakers, and together they are always rescuing someone. This couple may experience a plethora of problems and may even fight over who has it worse or sacrifices more. Martyrs can be perfectionists and may suffer from overwork or burnout, as they do not have proper boundaries. However, they will most likely find solace and comfort in their mutual suffering and sacrificing.

MARTYR–FOOL. The Fool's restlessness and lack of discipline can have financial consequences that only cause more suffering, self-sacrificing, and rescuing on the part of their Martyr partner. This may turn into a self-fulfilling prophecy for the Martyr and can eventually end in feelings of resentment and betrayal.

TYRANT–MARTYR. The more passive-aggressive Martyr may initially be drawn to the Tyrant as a caretaker of their needs and agenda. However, as the Tyrant becomes increasingly controlling and insecure, they may become too aggressive for the Martyr, who is quite sensitive and compassionate. They may try to get back at the Tyrant by overgiving and overspending as compensation for the Tyrant's controlling behavior. This can cause the Tyrant to feel threatened and engage in secrecy (hiding money and assets), aggression, and anger.

TYRANT–FOOL. The Tyrant may become triggered by the Fool's impulsive spending and irresponsible financial behavior. The two archetypes are polar opposites, as the

Fool is fearless around money and the Tyrant is the most fearful of all the types. As a result, the Fool will undoubtedly trigger the Tyrant's safety and control issues, and conflicts are inevitable.

TYRANT–TYRANT. This is a war waiting to happen. Think *War of the Roses*. Hide your weapons!

FOOL–FOOL. They will have a lot of fun together, have great adventures, and potentially go bankrupt, as they are risk takers and/or gamblers for whom making money is little more than a game.

Common Dominant/Passive Pairings

WARRIOR–INNOCENT. The Warrior will absolutely lead the couple's financial life. The Innocent will generally accept this arrangement because they seldom want to be responsible for the finances and long for the safety and security offered by their Warrior partner.

WARRIOR–VICTIM. The Warrior will be the family's financial manager in this pairing as well, but the Victim archetype will often complain about it and may even sabotage the relationship because of their propensity for living out self-fulfilling prophecies. If the Victim succeeds in sabotaging the couple's finances, they may blame the Warrior by saying that the Warrior was too controlling, or make some other justification, as they seldom claim responsibility.

WARRIOR–CREATOR/ARTIST. As with the Innocent pairing, the Warrior will be in charge of this couple's money matters. The Creator/Artist will generally be okay with this arrangement as long as they have some say when it comes to their lifestyle. The Creator/Artist is a lover of freedom, beauty, and creativity. If the Warrior does not recognize this or attempts to control their partner's freedom, trouble may ensue.

MARTYR–INNOCENT. Since the Martyr loves to take care of and rescue others, this can be a comfortable fit for both parties because both of them get their needs met easily. The Martyr may eventually become resentful, however, if their Innocent partner takes them for granted and does not give them the recognition and appreciation they crave.

MARTYR–VICTIM. This is similar to the Martyr/Innocent pairing, except in this case, both types can be passive-aggressive, and this can lead to financial conflict, blame, and resentment. Be very careful if you have this pairing!

MARTYR–CREATOR/ARTIST. Again, since the Martyr is happy to be the rescuer and caretaker, the Creator/Artist can just do his or her own thing. Since the Creator/Artist is detached and conflicted around money anyway, this works out well for them. However, the Martyr will often complain about this arrangement and may feel that they have to sacrifice and work hard while the Creator/Artist pursues their creative or spiritual path.

FOOL–INNOCENT. As the saying goes, "A fool and his money are soon parted." Unfortunately, in this pairing, it's usually the Innocent's money. This can be a financially challenging relationship because the Innocent is drawn in by the Fool's charm and naively trusts and believes in their ideas and schemes. Sadly, together they often experience great losses and challenges at the hand of the Fool, leaving the Innocent feeling let down and betrayed.

FOOL–VICTIM. Since the Victim is so often living out a self-fulfilling prophecy, they generally expect that bad things will happen to them anyway. It's no accident that these two end up together relatively frequently. The adventurous, charming Fool simply walks into the trap and unconsciously fulfills the Victim's prophecy. This pairing can also have big financial challenges and money conflicts.

FOOL–CREATOR/ARTIST. Since the Creator/Artist is not very money-oriented, they too are often happy to go along with the Fool's financial frivolity. The difference, however, is that the Creator/Artist is so detached from money that losing it does not necessarily derail them as it might the other archetypes. Also, the Creator/Artist's spiritual nature makes them more likely to forgive their Fool partner.

TYRANT–INNOCENT, –VICTIM, OR –CREATOR/ARTIST. The Tyrant will tend to rule over the money domain with an iron fist in all these archetypal pairings. In general, the passive types will not challenge this but may ultimately feel oppressed by the Tyrant, which will cause them to internalize their feelings and become nonconfrontational out of fear. Eventually, the lack of safety and intimacy may cause the more passive types to seek more emotionally and financially safe options, depending on their core self-esteem and risk tolerance.

Common Passive Types in Relationship Together

INNOCENT–INNOCENT. This pair is like the blind leading the blind. Neither partner wants to be in charge, and problems can arise as one or both will need to step up to prevent financial challenges.

VICTIM–VICTIM. This pair can be very challenged financially because they cannot easily move beyond the past. Stuck and resistant, they will tend to blame each other and experience many financial hurdles because of their own unconscious behaviors, for which neither partner is willing to take responsibility.

CREATOR/ARTIST–CREATOR/ARTIST. These two can have lots of fun together and possibly do quite well, whether or not they are financially successful. They may experience some challenges along the way, but as long as they both get to live freely and authentically, they can easily be content with less because neither cares much about money or the material world.

It is not uncommon to have more than one dominant money type influencing your relationship. The dominant money types in relationship play off of each other in ways that are either *complementary* or *conflicting*. When working with couples, I have found it useful to deal with the most challenging archetypes first and then move on to the other types. Often, when you resolve the core issues of one archetype, the issues related to the other types will also calm down.

In the case of Julia and Thomas, they have two distinct patterns that have repeatedly created conflict in their relationship. For example, Julia has aspects of the Warrior, Tyrant, and

Martyr, and when they all become activated, it can create more pressure and conflict over money. The roots of these are in her childhood, as mentioned earlier, but currently they are triggered when Julia feels financially afraid or abandoned, or when she has been overworking or caretaking others' needs at the expense of her own. When this happens, Thomas's Innocent and Victim archetypes can become activated. The Innocent archetype feels overwhelmed and uncertain about what do; then his Victim feels criticized, as though nothing he ever does is right or good enough (which is a pattern formed in his childhood). He has, however, learned how to access his Warrior by asking for help, advice, and support when he feels uncertain about what to do.

Thomas has also learned how to understand and respond, rather than to react, when he sees Julia's Martyr or Tyrant type show up. He knows this is not always about him and has learned to keep his reactions in check. Conversely, Julia has learned to not criticize Thomas and to more often acknowledge his positive efforts, which has helped him to repair his self-esteem. Both Julia and Thomas gently point out when they notice each other's more challenging types showing up. Now they can consciously and actively choose to support each other in order to improve the situation, rather than moving into the old habitual patterns that always made things worse. Together, they have begun to thrive, personally and financially, and their love and intimacy have blossomed to new levels.

EXERCISE
Our Relationship Money Patterns

1. Write down each of your primary money types (a score of five or more is a primary money type).

2. Write down the words associated with each type.
3. What money types do you have in common?
4. What money types cause you challenges?
5. Which behaviors, if any, are causing conflicts in your relationship?
6. Where did those behaviors come from — your mother, your father, or someone else?
7. Is the trigger you experience based on the past?
8. Now that you know this, how might you respond to each other moving forward?

Great job! Together, you are already learning how to communicate and support each other with greater understanding and compassion.

Chapter Four

CREATING A LANGUAGE OF FINANCIAL INTIMACY

Communication leads to community, that is,
to understanding, intimacy, and mutual valuing.

— ROLLO MAY, *Power and Innocence*

I define financial intimacy as the ability to openly and honestly communicate with our partner around money while safely expressing our hopes, fears, needs, and concerns with love and respect for the relationship's highest good. In addition to breaking old patterns, partners need to learn how to become truly financially intimate with each other. Financial intimacy is the key to, and foundation of, our sense of safety and security in our relationships. When we can create this, we model and pass this way of being down to our children as well. Learning how to use healthy language will significantly enhance the financial intimacy in your relationship. Whether we are married or in a committed relationship, our money issues and patterns often collide, creating conflict that can easily lead to disharmony. When this happens, larger problems may develop, since many couples do not have the communication skills necessary to manage their financial conflicts.

Before I tell you *how* to make these changes, I first want to help you to understand *why* we human beings tend to become so emotionally triggered and reactive around money. This is critical to understand because the reasons we react are far more complex than you might imagine. As I mentioned earlier, money is a core survival issue, not unlike our need for food; our money patterns and behaviors are hardwired in the brain and part of our basic biology. The work I do with both individuals and couples is based on years of research in the fields of neuroscience, neuroeconomics (the science of money and the brain), and behavioral finance (the study of financial behaviors). These are relatively new fields, but they provide valuable new information that is greatly helping us to understand our highly complex and mysterious relationship with money.

Understanding Our Complex Money Behaviors

Regardless of what you may believe, your spouse or partner does not behave irrationally when discussing money because they are irrational in any definitive way. Most likely, they also are not behaving that way to annoy or spite you. In fact, they probably do not understand their own irrational or contradictory behaviors around money any better than you do. The reason for this is simple: these behaviors are unconscious, and their origins lie in our basic biology and/or are rooted in the past.

While our spouse's behavior may not have anything to do with us, we can and do often trigger our partner without realizing it. When this happens, the pain of a long-forgotten past is suddenly a part of the present. What's more, the triggered behavior is often irrational and incongruous in the person we know and love, and it can cause a secondary reaction and spiral out of control from there. The next thing you know, one of you is asking, "What just happened here?" and you both feel mystified and bruised by the experience.

Here's an example dialogue that illustrates how these emotional triggers often occur. Stacy and Joe have been working with me on and off for a couple of years and have made huge improvements in their relationship with money, individually and in their marriage. They returned for a money coaching tune-up when they experienced conflict they couldn't resolve on their own, which was creating stress in their marriage.

DEBORAH: So what's going on with you two? You were doing great — what happened?

STACY: We were doing great until we hit a wall due to Joe's unemployment situation, which is making me feel really anxious about money.

JOE: I'm doing everything I possibly can, but as usual, Stacy thinks I'm not doing enough or doing it right, and she's constantly riding me! Like I want to be unemployed and not be able to support my family!

DEBORAH: Stacy, can you tell me if there is something else that is bothering you? What's your *real* fear?

STACY: I'm afraid it's always going to be like this. I'll be the one working the hardest, making most of the money. I want to be able to work less and spend more time with my children while they're still young! This is not the life I wanted, and I really resent Joe for not doing more to improve our circumstances.

DEBORAH: What does this circumstance remind you of?

STACY: It reminds me of how hard my mom worked and how abandoned I felt because she was always working and struggling financially.

DEBORAH: Great job. Now you've discovered what your real trigger is and why things have escalated so quickly. Your reaction is just that, a reaction rooted in the past.

STACY: Yes, and now *I'm doing the same thing to my kids*, which I swore I'd never do! It makes me so angry and sad.

DEBORAH: Joe, I sense you're also being triggered by the past. When you feel criticized by Stacy, what does that remind you of?

JOE: It reminds me of how my father treated me and how nothing I ever did was right or good enough. This feels the same way, and it makes me feel like I'm a failure.

DEBORAH: So tell me, are you in any real danger, financially speaking, right now?

STACY: Not really; we have some money set aside.

DEBORAH: Great! So perhaps we should focus on helping you to stay present and focused on what you want to create rather than reacting from the past. Because right now, you're okay and safe. Focus on knowing that. Also keep in mind that when you're fearful or stressed, you're more prone to being triggered and reacting. Next time you feel yourself becoming triggered, slow down and check in to see if what you're feeling is about something in the present or if it's from the past. Give yourself five minutes to reflect and respond, rather than react. It will make a huge difference.

This dialogue shows how money conflicts in the present may connect directly to past experiences, often those from childhood. The money conflicts and issues that you experience with your partner are not always about what they appear to be. There is often a root cause that lies beneath the apparent conflict. If you can discover it, you will be far less likely to become reactive with your partner and move into a negative spiral.

Here are a few questions you can ask yourselves when you or your spouse is feeling overly stressed or reactive regarding money and your finances:

1. Does this experience remind me (or my spouse) of a similar situation from childhood?
2. Am I secretly afraid that a negative past experience is going to repeat?
3. Am I secretly afraid that I will let somebody down (whether living or deceased) by my financial circumstances because of how I was raised?
4. Am I secretly afraid that I will be like somebody I don't want to be like (whether living or deceased) as a result of my financial circumstances?

Your answers to these questions can reveal that much of the force behind your reactions is coming from the past, and noticing this can often help to calm down your immediate feelings of stress. You can review your current circumstances for what they really are — events in the present that are happening right now, with no true direct connection to the past.

By the way, don't be surprised if the questions I listed above cause you or your spouse to experience strong emotions when answering them, particularly if this is the first time you have considered these kinds of questions. In most cases, you will experience a sense of relief after identifying the past experiences or decisions that are at play in your current circumstances. Occasionally, the act of reviewing your past can bring up such strong emotions that you may require the support of a qualified counselor or therapist. Make sure to get the help you need if this happens.

When you recognize the emotional threads that connect you both to your respective pasts, you will see that understanding, compassion, and communication are what you need most. These qualities will help you to love and support each other through your money issues and differences. Couples who fail to do this often create a self-fulfilling prophecy in which their greatest fears are realized.

The following is the exercise that I gave Stacy and Joe; I highly recommend it for all couples and their families.

EXERCISE
Love Tab

Get a large pad of sticky notes or a whiteboard from an office supply store and hang it on the wall somewhere easy to see and access. (The sticky notes are great because you can keep the best ones, but the whiteboard is more economical and environmentally friendly.)

At the top of the paper or whiteboard, write "Our Family's Love Tab." Below the title, across the top, write the names of all the members of your household. Underneath each name, everyone in the family gets to write whatever loving thoughts, appreciations, or acknowledgments they wish, daily. Here's an example:

OUR FAMILY'S LOVE TAB

(Appreciation and Acknowledgment)

Joe

U R the Bestest
Loved your extra help
Appreciated your support
   today
Thanks for cooking dinner!

Stacy

love u mommy!
Date night was FUN!
good job, Mom
You made my week

Sam

Good job, son!
Thanks for helping
You rock!
A for effort for cleaning
   your room

Katie

Thanks for helping me this
   a.m. Xo, Mom
We're proud of you!
Wow...

Clyde

You're the cutest!
XOXOXO!!!
First word...DA!
Kisses

A couple of weeks after our session, Joe called me to report that he'd received not one but two job offers! He took the one that felt like the best fit, rather than the higher-paying job, as he'd learned that this had sabotaged him in his previous jobs. Now, Stacy is working only three days a week. She is happy that she can work less and be with her children more, and that she is no longer repeating her childhood family dynamic. They invited me over to their house recently to visit their new baby. I was touched to see their Love Tab up on the wall, and their five-year-old son was writing sweet notes with happy faces to his parents and siblings. It's become a daily habit for everyone to write words of love and appreciation to each other. Such a simple thing, but it's changed their lives!

Every relationship experiences financial challenges or conflict at some point. Regardless of the causes of your financial issues, if your relationship is going through a difficult time, you most likely could use some new strategies to help guide you through this phase of your life. Here are seven financial survival steps that will truly help. Remember that now, more than ever, you need your relationship to provide a loving, supportive shelter from the storm that is occurring around you.

The Seven Relationship Survival Steps

1. Remember that your core money issues get triggered when you are under stress, but they did not originate in your marriage. They represent unhealed wounds from childhood (or perhaps from a previous relationship or marriage) that you mostly likely brought into the relationship. Have compassion for each other and learn how to understand each other's wounds from the past. Become more aware of how you trigger each other, and then try to avoid engaging in those behaviors.

2. It is so easy to focus on what's wrong that we often forget to remember what's good and right in our relationship. Make a list of what is working in your relationship and what you love about your partner. Share this openly with each other. There is nothing like hearing sincere words

of praise and appreciation to help soothe and calm our ruffled feathers or hurt feelings.

3. Most financial differences are due to a failure to effectively communicate our needs, fears, and grievances, which accumulate over time. Learn to talk openly, calmly, and without blame. If there is an issue that is seemingly irresolvable, seek the guidance of a trusted coach, therapist, minister, or spiritual counselor.

4. Respect each other, and either accept your differences or work together to resolve them. Don't let your differences destroy your relationship. With help and support, you can learn to honor these differences and perhaps even grow together because of them, rather than in spite of them.

5. During times of conflict, make a pact to not engage with each other until you have both calmed down. Take a walk, meditate, or turn to your spiritual Source for guidance and support through daily prayer and affirmation.

6. After you are able to be calm and present again, find a moment to consciously practice loving-kindness, compassion, and forgiveness. Never go to bed or leave mad! At the Money Coaching Institute, we teach and practice an ancient Hawaiian spiritual practice of reconciliation and forgiveness called Ho'oponopono, adapted by Morrnah Simeona, a healing priest, from the traditional Ho'oponopono practice to its modern-day use. I have witnessed and experienced miracles through the power of this simple process. I have seen families in crisis heal anger and wounds that had caused years of pain and destruction. I've witnessed profound healing between people who had not spoken in years. And I use this process in my everyday life with anyone I have any conflict

or disturbance with. I recommend that all couples use this as a ritual for healing their hurts, anger, or conflicts. Ho'oponopono can be conducted with your partner in person or remotely. I've found it to be equally effective either way. If you are working remotely, simply visualize your partner (or whomever) in your mind's eye and say the person's name out loud, followed by these words:

> I love you
> I'm sorry
> Please forgive me
> Thank you

Repeat the words like a mantra until you feel some release or opening in your heart. Continue to do this daily until you experience a shift in the relationship.

If your partner or spouse is open and receptive, do this process together. Begin by standing, facing each other, and holding hands. Look into each other's eyes and take turns repeating these words:

> I love you
> I'm sorry
> Please forgive me
> Thank you

Whether you are conducting this process remotely or while gazing into each other's eyes, be prepared for miracles to happen. It never ceases to amaze me how something so simple could be the cause of so many miracles!

But then, forgiveness itself is perhaps the most healing prescription available on the planet today, so no wonder!

7. Remain in partnership and continue to work together as a team. In many relationships, the moment when a partner becomes an opponent or adversary signals the beginning of the end of the relationship. Unfortunately, this may result from a subtle internal emotional shift or change in attitude that isn't apparent at first. If you find yourself polarizing your spouse, viewing him or her as a competitor or adversary, it's important to take immediate action to change your attitude. The same thing applies if you are on the receiving end of such an attitude from your spouse.

You and your spouse have to operate together as a team to be able to surmount the challenges that life throws at you. Teams can be effective and powerful even when the team members themselves are not perfect. Consider the following points for yourself and your spouse to help improve the quality of your teamwork:

- In what ways might my spouse's flaws and weaknesses (as I perceive them) actually be strengths? Are there any circumstances where these qualities have helped me or our family in ways that I haven't fully acknowledged?
- What is my spouse capable of doing that I am either unable or unwilling to do? How has this contributed to our relationship and our family?
- What am I grateful to my spouse for?
- What help does my spouse need that I am willing and qualified to provide?

- What help do I need that my spouse could provide?
- What areas do we need to handle better that either (or both) of us could step up and take care of?
- What reasonable expectations for change can I hold for my spouse or myself? What factors are unlikely to change?
- What activities do we, or could we, do together that we *both* enjoy and that help us to work together as a team?
- What unresolved conflicts do we have that are polarizing us? How can we move beyond these conflicts?
- What do I most appreciate about us together (not individually)? Together, what do we bring to the world that is special?

To succeed with this approach, both you and your spouse need to be committed to working together as a team. If you are trying to be a good team member while your spouse is indifferent, you will quickly find yourself feeling the betrayal of the Victim or the unsupported frustration of the Martyr.

It takes two!

Learning How to Talk about Money

Money is still a taboo subject in most families, or at the very least it's a highly emotional and triggering subject. We simply have never been given the tools, education, or modeling about how to talk about money. I used to think, when I was a financial advisor, that we just needed more financial education programs to be integrated into our education. As a money coach, however, I have learned that if we receive financial education without first learning how to talk about money and understand our money behaviors, the educational component itself falls short. Behavioral education and healthy communication are as important as financial education, if not more so.

While I am still a major advocate of financial literacy and education, the real problem is that we still don't know how to communicate about money. In fact, most of our money conversations, if we have them at all, are fraught with fear, anger, frustration, and blame. Without question, money is one of the most emotionally reactive subjects that couples engage in, and therefore it's a subject they often avoid or handle ineffectively.

Practicing Healthy Money Communication

Many people find the principles and tools developed by the Center for Nonviolent Communication helpful in establishing more positive communication behaviors. Located in New Mexico, the center is a global leader in helping people to learn and practice healthy communication techniques. The principles of nonviolent communication are simple and straightforward; anything that needs to be communicated between people *can be* communicated if done so in a healthy, clear, and effective manner. We all have the capacity to learn how to communicate this way, and learning these techniques is increasingly necessary if we are to live in greater peace and harmony with one another.

Fundamentally, nonviolent communication involves understanding that language both informs and communicates emotion. Communication steps over the line from providing information to causing harm when it is used to attack somebody or make him or her feel wrong. Nobody ever likes to feel wrong.

Questions such as "Why did you [mistake or harmful action]?" are unanswerable because nobody ever really knows why they make mistakes or errors in life. If they did, they'd do differently! What they do know is that you are angry and inviting them to quarrel with you.

However, nonviolent communication is not about stuffing your upsets and emotions away and never talking about them. It is about understanding how to communicate your needs and viewpoints in a manner that allows them to be heard by others. If you are angry, it is better to acknowledge your anger and fears as the subject of the conversation ("I'm feeling very angry and afraid") than to use innuendo or implications about the other person to express your feelings ("Can you explain to me why you only think about yourself?").

Here are some simple but highly effective ways to communicate about money using positive, nonblaming "I" statements to address your issues and concerns:

UNHEALTHY, TRIGGERING COMMUNICATION: "I was reviewing our finances and noticed that you spent money on things for yourself that were not in our budget, which makes me feel really angry and deceived."

HEALTHY COMMUNICATION: "Sweetheart, I'm feeling a bit worried about our finances and wondered if we could review our family budget and spending agreement together to help me feel safe."

UNHEALTHY, TRIGGERING COMMUNICATION: "Why did you spend so much money on gifts for the children? They already have everything they need! This is just plain foolish! What were you thinking?"

POSITIVE, HEALTHY COMMUNICATION: "I noticed that you went holiday shopping and was a bit concerned when I saw the bill. I thought we agreed on a budget. Can we talk about what happened for you when you went shopping?"

UNHEALTHY, TRIGGERING COMMUNICATION: "I feel like I work harder and harder to support our family, and you just keep spending more and more. Maybe you should become the breadwinner, and I'll stay home and shop!"

POSITIVE, HEALTHY COMMUNICATION: "Can we talk? I'm feeling sad and somewhat frustrated over our financial situation. Can we work together to create more of a savings plan? I really need your help with this."

Before engaging in a financial conversation, first check in with yourself to identify your needs and feelings. For example: "I'm feeling anxious and fearful about money. I need to feel more safe and in control of our family finances."

Next, approach your partner or spouse at an appropriate time and perhaps say, "I'm feeling somewhat fearful and anxious about our finances lately, and our spending habits are worrying me. I need some time to connect and talk with you about this so that together we can figure out a way to help me feel more financially safe and secure. Can we talk about this now or schedule a family money meeting sometime this week?"

Below is the basic model offered by the Center for Nonviolent Communication. It can help you and your partner to connect to your basic needs. According to their teaching, the most basic needs we all have are for "connection, physical well-being, safety, honesty, play, meaning, and autonomy."

This model is quite easy to use and involves learning how to empathetically listen and honestly express your feeling and needs. To use this model with your partner or spouse while discussing money, simply begin by honestly expressing your needs, observations, and feelings in the following manner.

Healthy Communication Frameworks:

FIRST, CLEARLY STATE YOUR OBSERVATIONS: "I've become aware that we are spending beyond our means lately."

NEXT, CLEARLY EXPRESS YOUR FEELINGS: "I feel concerned and feel that we're spiraling out of control around money, and it scares me."

THEN, CLEARLY EXPRESS YOUR NEEDS: "I need for us to sit down and make a plan and stick to it so that we don't end up with more debt than we can manage."

FINALLY, COMPLETE YOUR COMMUNICATION BY MAKING A REQUEST: "My request is that we meet sometime this week to work on this. Will you set aside the time, please?"

While you are honestly expressing yourself to your partner or spouse, he or she is to simply remain present and listen empathetically while observing your feelings and listening deeply to your needs.

Once you have completed your statement, your partner can respond by saying something like "Thank you for sharing your feelings with me. Is it okay if I take some time to think about this and respond more thoughtfully?" Another good response might be "I hear your concerns and can see that you're feeling triggered and fearful, so yes, I agree to sit down with you this weekend and work this out together. I love you and do not want you to feel alone or afraid around this."

Alternatively, your partner can express back to you his or her observations, feelings, needs, or requests — for example, "My observation is that when you get fearful around money, you hit the panic button and become reactive. How can I help you feel safe?"

Here are some examples of words that you can use to communicate your feelings when your needs are satisfied:

Affectionate	Excited	Inspired
Compassionate	Amazed	Amazed
Friendly	Animated	Awed
Loving	Ardent	Wonder
Openhearted	Aroused	**Joyful**
Sympathetic	Astonished	
Tender	Dazzled	Amused
Warm	Eager	Delighted
Confident	Energetic	Glad
	Enthusiastic	Happy
Empowered	Giddy	Jubilant
Open	Invigorated	Pleased
Proud	Lively	Tickled
Safe	Passionate	
Secure	Surprised	**Peaceful**
	Vibrant	Calm
Engaged	**Exhilarated**	Centered
		Clearheaded
Absorbed	Blissful	Comfortable
Alert	Ecstatic	Content
Curious	Elated	Equanimous
Enchanted	Enthralled	Fulfilled
Engrossed	Exuberant	Mellow
Entranced	Radiant	Quiet
Fascinated	Rapturous	Relaxed
Interested	Thrilled	Relieved
Intrigued		Satisfied
Involved	**Grateful**	Serene
Spellbound		Still
Stimulated	Appreciative	Tranquil
	Moved	Trusting
	Thankful	
	Touched	**Refreshed**
	Hopeful	Enlivened
		Rejuvenated
	Encouraged	Renewed
	Expectant	Rested
	Optimistic	Restored
		Revived

Here are some examples of words that you can use to communicate your feelings when your needs are not satisfied:

Afraid	Averse	Disquieted
Apprehensive	Animosity	Agitated
Dread	Appalled	Alarmed
Foreboding	Contempt	Discombobulated
Frightened	Disgusted	Disconcerted
Mistrustful	Dislike	Disturbed
Panicked	Hate	Perturbed
Petrified	Horrified	Rattled
Scared	Hostile	Restless
Suspicious	Repulsed	Shocked
Terrified		Startled
Wary	**Confused**	Surprised
Worried		Troubled
	Ambivalent	Turbulent
Angry	Baffled	Turmoil
	Bewildered	Uncomfortable
Enraged	Dazed	Uneasy
Furious	Hesitant	Unnerved
Incensed	Lost	Unsettled
Indignant	Mystified	Upset
Irate	Perplexed	
Livid	Puzzled	**Embarrassed**
Outraged	Torn	
Resentful		Ashamed
	Disconnected	Chagrined
		Flustered
Annoyed	Alienated	Guilty
	Aloof	Mortified
Aggravated	Apathetic	Self-conscious
Disgruntled	Bored	
Dismayed	Cold	
Displeased	Detached	
Exasperated	Distant	
Frustrated	Distracted	
Impatient	Indifferent	
Irked	Numb	
Irritated	Removed	
	Uninterested	
	Withdrawn	

Fatigued	Sad	Vulnerable
Beat	Depressed	Fragile
Burned-out	Dejected	Guarded
Depleted	Despair	Helpless
Exhausted	Despondent	Insecure
Lethargic	Disappointed	Leery
Listless	Discouraged	Reserved
Sleepy	Disheartened	Sensitive
Tired	Forlorn	Shaky
Weary	Gloomy	**Yearning**
Worn out	Heavy-hearted	
	Hopeless	Envious
In Pain	Melancholy	Jealous
	Unhappy	Longing
Agony	Wretched	Nostalgic
Anguished		Pining
Bereaved	**Tense**	Wistful
Devastated		
Grief	Anxious	
Heartbroken	Cranky	
Hurt	Distressed	
Lonely	Distraught	
Miserable	Edgy	
Regretful	Fidgety	
Remorseful	Frazzled	
	Irritable	
	Jittery	
	Nervous	
	Overwhelmed	
	Restless	
	Stressed out	

© 2005 by Center for Nonviolent Communication
(www.cnvc.org; cnvc@cnvc.org; 505-244-4041)

When we feel that we can openly and safely talk about our
wants and needs, and feel heard and met by our partner in this,
we begin to create the necessary foundation for love and intimacy

to deepen. Take a moment now to connect with your relationship with money by completing the exercise below.

EXERCISE
My Money Beliefs

Fill in the blanks with words that describe your feelings and beliefs about money.

1. I believe money is _____ .
2. When I think about money, I feel _____ .
3. When it comes to money, what I need most is _____ .
4. When it comes to money and our finances, what I need from you is _____ .

Financial Transparency and Honesty

When I was a child, I heard about a family that had adopted a little boy from a foreign land, where the boy had been raised in abject poverty and desperation. The adopting family found food hidden underneath his bed for months after they had adopted him. Even though he was now safe and loved, his fear of starvation and lack was so great that he couldn't trust his current circumstances and continued to hoard food for many months.

Like the adopted boy, many of us have covert financial aspects of ourselves that don't trust that we will be honored, safe, taken care of, and loved. We create secret bank accounts, hide purchases, and may never be fully forthcoming with our spouse about our own money story and true needs.

You can resolve these issues only by creating the safety within your relationship for the truth to exist. Everybody has a past money story, sorrows, and shadows that need to be healed. Encourage financial honesty in your relationship by openly discussing financial issues, holding a space for your partner's (and your own) fears and concerns, and asking for the same from your partner.

Here is an exercise for you and your partner to do individually that can help you to identify and resolve some of the money shadows that may inhibit the financial honesty and, therefore, financial intimacy in your relationship.

EXERCISE

Personal Inventory

1. Do a personal inventory to determine what secret shame, anger, fear, or concerns you are holding. Make a list and share it.
2. How are these hidden aspects showing up in the present? Do you compensate by making purchases you don't need, overspending, or somehow depriving yourself? Are you enforcing any of these factors (or their opposites) with your spouse or children?
3. What steps can you take toward resolving these issues that feel safe to you?
4. If you took these steps, how might it improve your circumstances and financial intimacy?

This is not an easy exercise. It requires you to examine your own money shadow, which is not pleasant for anybody. It also involves engaging your spouse regarding his or her money shadow, which has its own challenges. For this exercise, I recommend that you respect each other's boundaries and allow each other to complete the exercise on your own. However, the goal is to improve both the financial honesty and intimacy in your relationship. If you or your partner needs to communicate further or suggest any changes at the conclusion of this exercise, please listen to each other with love, compassion, and acceptance.

Chapter Five

MANAGING YOUR MONEY
CONVERSATIONS

Love is the only gold.

— ALFRED, LORD TENNYSON, *Becket*

Learning how to communicate effectively about money
is key to the success of all intimate relationships. Unfortunately,
conversations about money are so highly emotionally charged
that many couples may wish to avoid them altogether. This chapter explores how to navigate through your conversation about
money and offers some ground rules that can help ensure win-
win financial and emotional outcomes. To begin, it will be helpful to establish a new baseline for communicating, one that isn't
about money, per se, but that addresses what you both came to
give and to receive in your relationship. Speaking your needs out
loud will help you to become aware of and acknowledge each

other's intrinsic needs. As you work together to develop a deeper awareness of your individual needs and desires, you will open the space between you, allowing both of you to expand your willingness to be truly open and vulnerable with each other.

Each relationship is its own container of giving and receiving. When two people feel safe enough to fully show up and express all that they came to give, their relationship container overflows and they experience greater inner and outer abundance. The key is reciprocity. Are you and your partner fully conscious of what you each give to and receive from one another? Do you openly acknowledge and appreciate each other? Unfortunately, many couples become less conscious of this over time.

If you or your partner is withholding or constricted in the way you give, your relationship might be experiencing a corresponding shortage. This kind of thinking requires a whole new understanding of "accounts receivable." For example, if money is not flowing well in your lives, it is possible that the giving or receiving between you and your partner is out of balance. Are you a self-proclaimed giver who is hard to give to because you are uncomfortable receiving? Or do you feel so entitled to receiving that you have neglected to consider how you can reciprocate by giving back occasionally? These two elements represent equally important aspects of our basic human needs. It is essential to take a closer look at the accounts receivable in your relationship to determine how balanced or imbalanced you have become. This doesn't mean you need to keep track or even that the giving and receiving should be fifty-fifty. Sometimes one person in the relationship needs more than the other, and that's healthy. When you are balanced, you will both feel and experience it energetically as a deficit or surplus — preferably a surplus!

Accounts Receivable — Relationship Barometers

DEFICIT GIVING — Occurs when one person is overdoing or overgiving to another. This leads to irritability, resentment, and burnout.

OVER-RECEIVING — Occurs when one person in the relationship feels overly entitled, is self-centered, and ignores the needs of their partner.

UNDER-RECEIVING — Occurs when one or both partners are shut down emotionally and are therefore no longer open to receiving. This leads to emotional depletion, suffering, and self-sacrifice.

DEFICIT SPENDING — Occurs when both parties are not getting their needs met and are low on energy, enthusiasm, and passion. Whatever couples are giving at this point may feel more like an effort, and both parties may be running on empty, emotionally and financially.

SURPLUS SPENDING — This is the optimal place for your relationship. When both people are consciously giving and receiving, they experience comfort and joy. They feel taken care of, close, and intimate because their needs are met. As a result, they are both able to give and receive openly and abundantly. Their cup runneth over; the more they give, the more they receive. This kind of conscious reciprocity allows the natural cycle of giving and receiving to be self-perpetuating and regenerative.

Giving and receiving are wonderful forms of generosity that are part of our intrinsic nature, just as loving is. The only reason why we might withhold our giving or our love is if we feel fearful or resentful or we are holding emotional pain. The same is true of our inability to receive, which stems from being shut down emotionally or feeling unworthy. The better the energy and flow between two people, the easier it is to attract and maintain a healthy relationship, personally and financially.

EXERCISE

Giving and Receiving

Answer the following questions in your journal:

1. What did you come to give to your marriage or relationship?
2. What do you need to receive from this marriage or relationship?

After you complete the exercise, share your lists, and ask your partner these questions:

1. What did you learn about me that you didn't know?
2. How will knowing this help you (and us) to be more aligned?
3. Do I allow the space for you to fully give? If not, what would you like me to improve?
4. Are you currently receiving all that you need? Is there an area I can improve upon?

To be truly intimate, it is important to know, rather than assume, what your partner needs to give and to receive. When you become aware of and address each other's true needs, your relationship will begin to flourish. If you don't know what your partner's true needs are, how can you possibly ever meet them?

Couples often miss the mark in this area. For example, one couple I worked with was close to divorce because the husband, while highly successful, was oblivious to his wife's true needs. Jorge and Maria had been married for over ten years when I met them. They had started out as many couples do, with very little money. Over time, Jorge, who was very financially driven, had become highly successful running his biotech company. They were multi-millionaires and had everything materially that one could ever ask for. The problem was, in Jorge's mind there was never enough. So while Jorge wheeled and dealed, amassing more and more wealth, he all but abandoned his wife and children, both physically and emotionally. He was frequently away on business and was disconnected from the true needs of his wife.

When Maria told him that she wanted a divorce, he was shocked. He told her, "I've given you everything — look at this house, this life. How could all this not be enough?" Her response was, "I didn't get married to this house or this life — I married you, and you barely exist in this relationship. I'm lonely, the kids barely know you, and this isn't the life I ever wanted. It's the one you wanted. Well, you can have it."

Maria's primary archetype is the Creator/Artist, so money was not what motivated her. She appreciated their life and home, but she longed for intimacy and connection, which Jorge was too busy to provide her with. Maria felt that while she had not changed much over the years, Jorge was no longer the man she had married. After a couple of months of working together, Jorge began to realize that he had allowed his Warrior archetype to grow into a full-blown Tyrant. His critical and unloving father had always told him that he would never amount to anything. He was cold and indifferent to Jorge. In addition, Jorge's mother was passive and did not stand up on her son's behalf, which made Jorge angry as a boy. Jorge's unconscious desire to prove his father wrong drove him to become a Tyrant, just like his father. It is not uncommon for the unresolved issues we have with one of our parents (usually the one we resist the most) to become our own issues as well. Another key factor in Jorge's neglect of Maria was that he projected his unresolved anger toward his mother onto his wife, which caused him to become indifferent to her needs.

At my recommendation, Jorge and Maria entered into couples therapy in addition to their money coaching work with me. I am happy to report that they are still together and are quite happy. Jorge began to realize that he had more than enough money but had missed the boat as a father and husband. He decided to sell his company and focus on his home life for a while, while the family lived off his investments. He and Maria are planning to start a family foundation to help make a difference in the lives of single mothers, a cause close to Maria's heart.

Making Friends with Money

Many people have an angry or unhappy relationship with money but fail to notice how this impacts their lives. Money can be a good friend and resource that can help us to create financial peace and security, which we all innately desire. Although money is not the answer to all of our life's problems, it can and does serve a great purpose. So, wouldn't it be better if we befriended money, got to know it better, and even learned how to work and play with it more effectively?

You see, money is not the problem any more than it is the solution. We tend to equate having money with getting our needs met and not having it as not getting our needs met. Aside from our basic needs, money shouldn't be included in the formula of what we require to meet our needs. If you look closely at your

"Giving and Receiving" lists, you'll find that in most cases, what you indicated that you need to give and receive has little to do with money.

If we dislike someone or have conflicted feelings about him or her, eventually that person will take the hint and go away or begin to avoid us. Energetically, the same thing can happen with money. If we store up enough negativity around money, it can become scarce and create challenges in our financial life.

Also, if you or your partner secretly believes that you don't deserve more money or, perhaps, that money itself is bad, you can unconsciously create a reality that reflects this belief system. So it's important to clear out any negative thoughts or beliefs you may be holding about money or your personal finances so that you can create a more positive field from which to attract and sustain the financial reality you both desire.

Developing a Mindful Money Practice

Advances in quantum theory, quantum physics, and quantum mechanics are making it more and more likely that we will one day understand the relationship between mind and matter and begin to develop its untapped potential. David Bohm, perhaps the greatest quantum physicist of our time, believed that consciousness is far more than just information stored in the brain; information itself enters into consciousness and is part of the whole. For Bohm, "Consciousness...involves awareness, attention, perception, acts of understanding, and perhaps yet more."

This thinking strongly parallels the archetypal journey we must travel from unconsciousness to awareness; from awareness to conscious attention and intention, increased personal observation, and perceptivity; and finally to understanding, compassion, and right action. When we travel this path, we do seem to be able to tap into the field of our greater potentiality, personally and financially. In my view and experience, this is the space where we manifest our highest potential and miracles are born.

We now know that not only do our thoughts matter, but they *are* matter; and as such, they possess organizing potential. Therefore, our thoughts, words, intentions, and actions have real power, which is why we must learn how to choose and use them wisely. It is both essential and critical to maintain good mental and spiritual "hygiene" to keep the field of your potentiality clear from negative thoughts that might adversely impact or create blocks to your personal and financial well-being.

Unfortunately, our negative associations around money can adversely affect our experience with it, and they may even unconsciously sabotage us and our relationships. Some of these negative thoughts or beliefs may have been formed in early childhood, due to experiences long past, and have taken up residence inside our subconscious mind.

Use the following intention and affirmation to help clear your mind and your relationship of any negative thoughts or beliefs that either of you may hold around money. Repeat this affirmation daily to help improve your relationship with money.

Mindful Money Clearing Affirmation

I cleanse my mind of any and all negative thoughts and associations about money. I accept money as a positive force and ally in my life.

I release and forgive all my past mistakes around money.

I release and forgive my partner's mistakes as well.

I accept responsibility for myself and my financial well-being.

I believe that we live in an abundant universe and that this
abundance is available to us right here and right now.
I release any obstacle, doubt, or limitation that exists in
my mind.
I am free of the illusion of lack.
I know there is more than enough, I have enough, I am
enough.
I am willing and ready to receive financial grace and
abundance with ease, openness, and a grateful heart.

Growing Your Relationship with Appreciation

When we appreciate someone, it is important to show them
that we care and that we value them. Like any financial asset we
choose to invest in with hopes that it will appreciate over time,
our relationships will also grow in value and worth as we consciously and actively appreciate them. Your relationship is far
more valuable than any asset you will ever own. When you do
not actively appreciate your partner, the relationship may lose
value over time, which could cost you, in some cases, half of
what you own, should you lose it. So investing time and energy
into learning how to communicate about money is an excellent
way to avoid the unnecessary loss of your relationship or financial
assets.

During a recent session with Sid and Linda, a couple I'm
working with, the question arose as to whether there is a difference between gratitude and appreciation — and if so, what is
it? In the thick of the discussion, Sid pulled out his iPhone and
searched the Internet for what others may have shared about this
question. We found answers that pretty much mirrored our own
perspectives. One common distinction we found is that gratitude
is the base from which appreciation grows and flourishes, if we're

paying attention. Therefore, we can be grateful for something in our lives without appreciating it.

The subtle shift from gratitude to appreciation involves being more present, thoughtfully aware, and active in reflecting on our reasons for feeling grateful about something or someone. Through present-moment awareness, we begin to generate feelings of appreciation. For example, we can be grateful for having food on our table. However, we can go further and appreciate its beauty, fragrance, taste, nutrition, and preparation. We move beyond thankfulness as we consciously recognize the value that food adds to our lives. In fact, one definition of the word *appreciation* is "recognition of the quality, value, significance, or magnitude of people and things."

When we live appreciatively, we experience our partner as someone who makes us feel brighter, lighter, happier, more inspired, energized, and loved. Gratitude and appreciation turn what we have into enough, and then some. They turn denial into acceptance, chaos into order, confusion into clarity. They can turn a meal into a feast, a house into a home, a stranger into a friend, and our relationship into a sacred sanctuary.

EXERCISE

What I Love and Appreciate about You

Do this process with your partner.

Begin by making a list of what you love and appreciate about each other. Then prepare a special dinner together in honor of your relationship. Light some candles, and maybe even wear something you know your partner will appreciate seeing you in. Before you begin to enjoy your meal together, read your "What I Love and Appreciate about You" lists out loud to each other. (You might want to have a box of tissues nearby, as one or both of you will probably cry. These are good tears, however, of happiness and connection that perhaps you haven't felt for a while.)

The Big Money Topics

As you build a foundation of trust and intimacy, it will become easier to manage financial conversations that you might previously have found challenging and possibly even avoided. Below is a list of important money conversations that I strongly feel every couple should have.

SPENDING VERSUS SAVING. Many couples have different patterns of spending and saving. If you and your mate fight about saving versus spending, it might be better to pool your money for your fixed household expenses and split the leftovers. This will allow you both the freedom to spend or save, depending on your needs. The downside of this is that if one of you is a spender and spends all your money, and then expects the other to share their savings with you, this can lead to problems. If saving is difficult for one of you, perhaps agree that 50 percent of their portion of the leftovers is automatically invested out of their paycheck or into their 401(k). This is a common scenario in Fool/Warrior relationships.

DEBT. This can be a loaded conversation, depending on your primary money types. In general, Fool archetypes are the biggest debtors because they have the highest risk tolerance. But Creator/Artists and Warriors can be comfortable with debt as well, to a point, especially if it's for business expansion or a pet project, such as renovating their home. However, if your partner is a strong Tyrant archetype, you might want to curtail your credit card purchases.

TO MINGLE OR NOT: YOURS, MINE, AND OURS. Many people enter into relationships with their own money and have no intention or desire to mingle it with their partner's money. Not everyone is clear and up front about this in the beginning, however. I have worked extensively with couples where one partner feels dejected or rejected when the other does not want to share or mingle money. This can create a lot of discomfort for both parties, and there is no right or easy answer. I recommend that couples consider a prenuptial conversation first and agree on the terms. If either or both of you are still uncomfortable or unhappy, resolve this before you formalize your agreement legally. In my experience, the dissatisfied partner will not get any happier over time, in which case your relationship will most likely become a time bomb. No, you will not change his or her mind, and the more you press this issue, the worse it tends to become, because your partner may begin to question your motives. When you truly love someone, it is important to not let money be the issue that derails your relationship. If there's conflict or insecurity, work to resolve it and, if necessary, get help and support.

Inheritance Issues

With the largest wealth transfer in history taking place over the next twenty years, inheritance issues are increasingly a source of significant conflict among couples and their families. People seldom realize that inherited money often comes with a fair amount of emotional baggage. For example, after the loss of a parent or other loved one, people are often still grieving or have feelings of guilt about receiving an inheritance that is associated with the loss. This may prevent them from enjoying their inheritance. Also, some people feel protective of their inherited money and can feel an enormous sense of responsibility for managing it well or in agreement with the deceased's wishes.

We all know stories of the "spoiled little rich girl" or boy who inherits money and goes on to live a narcissistic lifestyle of parties, drugs, and excess. In my experience, however, there are far more people with inherited wealth who live very different, quietly wealthy lives. In fact, if you knew them, you might witness their feelings of anxiety, unworthiness, guilt, or discomfort with their wealth. People often say, "Oh, I wish I had *their* problems," but if they looked closer, they might think twice. Sudden wealth seldom makes people happier, and in many cases it simply increases their fears, anxiety, and stress. In my work with couples, I always ask them to give the spouse with the inheritance some space to grieve and get accustomed to his or her new money, especially if it's a large inheritance.

In addition, I believe that inherited wealth should be kept as separate property. That does not mean you shouldn't share your wealth with your partner, but one should never automatically *assume* that it should be mingled or shared. There may be legal stipulations that prevent mingling, or there may be a verbal agreement or pact in place. For example, my client Melanie's grandmother left her a small inheritance, and before she died, she specifically asked Melanie to keep the money for herself as a nest egg. She told Melanie, "Every woman and wife needs some money of her own. This money is for you." Melanie had some feelings of guilt about this initially, but after the work we did together, we all agreed that this was the right way for Melanie to honor her grandmother and their agreement.

Beliefs about Credit and Debt

Many couples develop problems due to very different beliefs and risk tolerances around the use of credit and debt. This is a common problem that can create trust issues if not handled properly. Your and your partner's comfort levels regarding credit cards and debt are usually determined by inherent differences in risk tolerance. Some people were raised in families where credit cards were never used and debt was considered bad. Others were raised in families where cash was seldom seen and credit cards were used to pay for everything. Some of these families paid their credit card bills in full every month, and others accumulated large debts. It is obvious that many people today overuse their credit cards and have more debt than is healthy or advisable. However, not all debt is created equal, and there are plenty of legitimate reasons to use credit rather than cash.

The problems that couples invariably run into with regard to credit and debt have to do with power and control based on fear. For example, Kevin came to see me because his wife, Paola, would go into a tirade every time he used his credit card. She forbade him to use it because, according to her, he kept getting them into serious debt. When I asked him what he generally used credit for, he replied, "Mostly my business, especially when we have cash-flow issues."

In fact, he had less than $20,000 associated with a business line of credit, which is not that high for the type of business he is in. Nonetheless, his wife was livid about it and was threatening to leave him. Initially, he went through the money coaching process alone in one of my intensive workshops. He learned a great deal about his own patterns and encouraged Paola to take the workshop, which turned out to be life altering for her. Together they realized that they were locked in a battle of the archetypes in which Paola's Innocent, Martyr, and Tyrant types were in combat with Kevin's Warrior, Fool, and Magician types. Paola's primary archetypes are Innocent-Martyr, and she seeks security and rescue but is also a caretaker and prone to self-sacrificing. Debt is very uncomfortable for her, and her Martyr felt betrayed and burdened by the debt that Kevin had accumulated. This activated her shadow Tyrant archetype, who became angry and controlling, largely out of financial fear and insecurity. The truth is, however, that Kevin's debt was not inappropriate. In fact, it is often necessary to use credit to stay in business. But Paola is an Innocent and had no understanding of business cash-flow and credit issues. To her, using credit was akin to "cheating" on her. I worked with Kevin and Paola to help them to better understand their patterns and to become more compassionate about their differences. They were able to make new agreements and now can talk openly and negotiate their money differences calmly from the heart.

Insurance

I've coached many couples over disputes regarding insurance, especially life insurance and long-term care insurance. I fought with my own husband about this as well (and I won!). Basically, it comes down to this: If you love your partner and your family, for very little money you can give them peace of mind, knowing that should you get hit by a bus, they will be able to afford to live the same, or at least a similar, lifestyle for a while — or, if you can afford it, maybe forever. What's the big deal? Just do it. It is the right and loving thing to do. Here are some steps you can take to ensure that your loved ones will be okay:

- Buy life insurance. Term insurance is very cheap, depending on your age and health. At a minimum, if you can afford it, get enough to pay off the house and cover your income loss while you still have children at home or in college.
- Look into long-term care insurance so that your spouse or children can afford to have you properly cared for in the event of a long-term illness. Policies with home health care options are the best.
- Create a living will with a state-approved medical directive so that your family can manage your care in the manner you wish in the event you are unable to communicate on your own behalf.
- Get a proper will and/or trust made up so that your family can settle your estate properly without any legal issues. Families can be torn apart by legal disputes, and believe me, it happens every day.

The care and attention you put into planning for your family now will allow them to live with your loving financial support long after you're gone. Trust me, they will remember you with gratitude, rather than sadness or regret, for their entire lives.

Aging Parents

This topic is fraught with emotional and practical issues. Having the money conversation about aging parents can be as charged and challenging as having the money conversation *with* aging parents as well as all the other family members who are affected by the decisions made. A group money coaching session, similar to couples coaching, is often helpful; each shares what they bring to give and what they need to receive.

Those who will be involved need to form an understanding and appreciation of each other's special skills, talents, abilities, time availability, and proximity, to prepare them to plan for the myriad needs of aging parents. Setting clear responsibilities, determining boundaries, and creating a plan of accountability is important in establishing and maintaining trust in the family. Of major importance is management of the aging parents' money, including cash flow, assets, a spending plan, debt, and taxes.

Insurance needs have to be considered; this can include property insurance, Medicare, Medicare Supplemental, long-term care insurance, and Medicaid.

Housing is a key issue — where will the aging parents reside? Who will be nearby, willing and able to help? If a parent is moved into the home of a family member who lives with a spouse or partner, what might be the impact on the couple's relationship?

Elder abuse is a concern, and it doesn't just involve mistreatment by family members or caregivers. It can occur in acts of fraud and deceit by con artists who try to separate the elderly from their money. Who will be in charge of ensuring that the aging parents are not victimized?

The estate plan should be in place, and this includes much more than can be covered in a short paragraph. Suffice it to say that taking care of business for the end of life is much easier when done well in advance, and it often requires the assistance of properly credentialed and licensed professionals who specialize in this area.

Retirement

Retirement is another ripe topic laden with potential challenges. Retirement is not just about money decisions; it includes lifestyle, time management, individual and shared interests, health, nutrition, legal, tax, estate, and other decisions. How will decisions be reached? Who will be responsible for which decisions? How will a common ground be reached? Does the couple have a dream to share, or do they have differing visions of how this phase of life may unfold?

Many changes can occur in this phase of life, including where to live, how to live, who will be nearby, what to do about those we may be leaving, how to occupy our time, how to avoid boredom, what's next in life, and much more. All of these issues need to be openly discussed and planned for if you hope to successfully retire one day. Steven Shagrin, a money coach who's also a Certified Financial Planner and Registered Life Planner, and someone to whom I frequently refer clients, offers this great advice:

> Once you have a mutual design in mind for your retirement, then you need to determine how much it might cost and see if there are enough financial resources to cover it all. If not, what will be cut and who will make that decision? Who might be called upon to continue employment in order to bring needed income to the family? The best way to deal with these financial matters is to commit to having meaningful money conversations on a regular basis. Take the financial issues covered here, sit down with your partner, and discuss how you wish to address each issue together. Don't delay or avoid these subjects as most couples do. In the end, you will be grateful for taking time to prepare for the cycles and changes that life brings.

Part of the way we can value and appreciate our relationships is to take the proper actions to ensure that we take care of those we love, no matter what. Just make a plan and do what you can!

Chapter Six

COMMON MONEY TRAPS
AND ISSUES

When money is seen as a solution for every problem,
money itself becomes the problem.

— RICHARD J. NEEDHAM

Our relationships are where we are forced, sometimes kicking and screaming, to surrender our mask and be willing to be totally vulnerable and seen, possibly for the first time.
As we shed our projections of what we had hoped for and begin to
accept each other and our circumstances as they truly are, we can
experience authentic love, rather than romantic love, and greater
acceptance of ourselves and our partners. This does not mean we
need to resign ourselves to our circumstances. We can and should
continue to hope and strive for better, but do so with an attitude
of acceptance and gratitude for what we already have that is good
and right — that makes the journey more beautiful and, yes, even
more tolerable.

When we are in harmony with money, we tend to feel safe and secure in the moment and hopeful for the future. The same is true when we feel in harmony with our spouse or partner: all is safe and secure in the world, and we feel connected to our hopes and dreams for the future. Unfortunately, the minute we become emotionally triggered around money, our internal dynamics can quickly shift from safe and secure to fearful and anxious. This can cause us to project our fears and anxieties onto our mate. With little or no warning, all those wonderful feelings of harmony and connectedness disappear. What's more, our feelings and contentment can easily flip like a switch. So what happens? What causes these sudden shifts and triggers in our feelings and emotions? Money traps, that's what!

Identifying Common Money Traps

We often mistakenly believe that more money is the cure to fixing or changing whatever isn't working in our life. And our tendency to focus on money as the problem and/or solution is only a clever distraction from looking at the *real* problem. It is naive to believe that money can somehow magically solve our life's problems. In fact, acquiring more money without also learning to understand and resolve our inner money dynamics frequently leads to even greater problems, as too few of us are prepared for the emotional, social, and practical consequences of wealth. With this in mind, we can address the issues most effectively by first exploring our internal landscape rather than diving head first into the pursuit of money, which is filled with booby traps.

When we feel financially safe and secure with our mate, we can easily relax and allow ourselves to be truly open and vulnerable. Unfortunately, many couples do not have this kind of intimacy and often fall into what I call money traps. The following are some of the most common *money traps* that I have seen:

- Using money as a form of control or manipulation
- Failure to understand each other's money fears and triggers
- Misunderstanding each other's financial wants and needs
- A clash in core values over what is important
- Unclear financial agreements and priorities
- Assuming unconscious roles (such as Dependent and Caretaker)
- Procrastinating or withholding pertinent financial information

Here are some ways to avoid these issues, all of which are covered in this book:

- Get to know each other's money types early in your relationship.
- Talk openly about your issues, fears, and concerns about money.
- Make clear agreements about how to handle money together as a couple.
- Never use money as a means of buying or withholding love.
- Take responsibility for your own financial well-being.
- Deal with money issues as they arise so that they don't become a source of resentment.

I also recommend these simple practical tips for dealing with money that will allow you to work together as a team to co-create the financial life you desire:

- Create a monthly household budget.
- Make joint decisions about what to do with the leftovers (spend it, save it, invest it).

- Establish a monthly allowance for each of you to spend or save, as you individually desire.
- Share the financial responsibilities, and divide up the tasks or take turns.
- Have a monthly money meeting to discuss and clear up any unfinished or new money business.
- Create a list of goals and dreams to work on together, and have fun with it.
- Acknowledge each other in positive ways for keeping agreements.

You can create the financial life you both want and deserve by understanding and supporting each other to be financially aware and empowered.

Moving from Blame to Forgiveness

Financial mistakes and setbacks happen. They're a part of life and a part of our growth and learning. When a financial loss or hardship occurs, it's not unusual to want to blame something or someone in order to cope with our feelings. Anger and blame can be a way of feeling in control, but they really only leave us feeling victimized and powerless.

Today, many couples are also blaming themselves or each other for their financial challenges, thinking, "If only I had done this" or "I can't believe I did that" or "What was I thinking?!" This kind of blame only fuels our fear, anger, and resentment and deepens the negative charge we have around the problem.

Let's face it, not all our money problems can be blamed on our financial circumstances alone. Some of us are grappling with old habits and patterns that existed long before the global financial crisis. True, financial crisis can make our circumstances considerably worse, but I would argue that the conditions for any financial crisis are often present long before the crisis occurs. Along with their financial challenges, couples are being given a new opportunity to rethink and revise their way of being in relationship with money.

Part of our work as adults is to realize that the subject of money is the last taboo and greatly needs to be explored and healed. In doing so, we can make clearer and more informed choices that better serve us and will help us to create a better future for ourselves and our children. We can no longer afford to take the ostrich approach to money or to be financially impulsive or avoidant.

Clearing the Past

Forgiveness is a great tool for releasing negative thoughts and feelings, which can be toxic and counterproductive. We are all looking for peace — peace of mind, body, and spirit — right? In order to find it, we need to examine our own responsibility in the situation and own our role in it. Once we have forgiven ourselves, we can more easily move forward to forgive others who have hurt or harmed us. Here are some key points to keep in mind when working through your forgiveness process:

1. Forgiveness is first and foremost for you. It is about taking back your power so that you can see and receive the good around you.
2. Forgiveness allows you to shift your perspective on what is happening. Recognize that your primary distress is coming from the hurt feelings and thoughts that are plaguing you, not what offended or hurt you ten minutes — or ten years — ago. Whether you are experiencing the loss of a job, your home, or your retirement savings, this

loss is the real issue, not who did it to you. Grieving a loss is an important process in and of itself, but forgiveness is the first step. Anger often denies us access to the pain of loss. Forgiveness will help you to clear the anger and resentment so that you can begin to feel the loss.

3. Forgiveness does not mean that you have to make up with the person. They don't even have to know, because it's not about them. Forgiveness offers you the opportunity to be at peace with the situation. This can be as simple as forgiving the investment company that managed your 401(k), or Wall Street, or your mortgage broker. Make a list and forgive them so that you can be free of this energetically and emotionally.

4. Remember that forgiveness is a process. It's not always easy, and healing takes time. Be gentle with yourself and allow yourself to go through your own process. I recommend writing a forgiveness letter to get your feelings on paper. Through writing, you can express your feelings openly, either to the person who wronged you or even to yourself. You do not have to give the letter to the person you are forgiving; it is part of your own process for letting go and creating your "forgiveness story."

Ultimately, forgiveness is a step toward spiritual and emotional expansion. It allows you to create the space for letting go of negative thoughts and feelings so that you can be free of the past and move forward to create the next chapter of your life.

Overcoming Your Money Traps

Over the years, I've received many cries for help from people who were in despair over their financial circumstances, but one couple in particular really moved me. Here's Elise and Robert's story:

Elise considered herself to be a very private person and had always had difficulty asking for help. She had stopped opening the bills and had stopped making timely payments because she simply could not manage her financial fear, anxiety, and shame. She knew she was sabotaging her family's financial well-being but was too embarrassed and ashamed to get help. Finally, her husband stepped in and said, "We cannot keep going like this; we are at our breaking point and need help and support." When they contacted me, I worked with them to understand their money traps and helped them to create a system for getting on track, personally and financially. Elise was an Innocent money type and was so overwhelmed and anxious about money that she had become financially frozen. In short, she was unconsciously sabotaging their financial life due to unresolved feelings of unworthiness and shame. She had silently begun to believe that she didn't deserve her husband or her family and was spiraling out of control. Her husband, Robert, only discovered this problem when the power was turned off. It wasn't because they didn't have the money to pay the bills. It was due to the unresolved emotional issues that manifested in the couple's combined unhealthy money behaviors.

Elise's Money Story

When Elise was a young girl, her family was relatively well-off and had all it needed and more. Her parents gave her everything she wanted and loved her dearly. She felt safe, secure, and happy.

One day, when she was eight years old, she was about to go on a field trip with her class, and her parents gave her $100 to buy herself lunch and some souvenirs. She was so happy to be given so much money and responsibility that she showed the others on the bus. Upon hearing about and seeing the money, her teachers became very reactive and took her money away and told her that it was "inappropriate" for an eight-year-old to have been given so much money. They chastised and shamed her in front of her class. Then, when they returned to school, the teachers called her parents and did the same to them. It was never discussed again.

Shortly after this, the family moved to another state, where Elise had more contact with cousins who had considerably less money than her family. They constantly criticized and teased her for being a spoiled brat who got everything she wanted. This made her feel ashamed, confused, and guilty for having more than others.

Within a couple of years, her father's business went bankrupt due to the economy, and they had to move from their beautiful home to an apartment and a much different financial reality. Her cousins told her that she "got what she deserved." Elise never spoke with anyone about these very conflicting and disturbing events and messages that she had received when she was young. She merely internalized the messages and felt that they were true.

As an adult, she felt overwhelmed and ashamed when she and Robert began to accumulate more money due to his business success. The old unhealed and unresolved wounds began to resurface, and as they did, Elise began to unconsciously sabotage their financial well-being. Having more than others was simply not safe for her. As I worked with Elise to understand and resolve this conflict, Robert was able to understand and forgive her behaviors, which, if left unmanaged, would have destroyed their financial life and their marriage. Robert was loving and compassionate, and together they healed their relationship and went on to establish new agreements and systems to manage their financial life.

Though difficult, acknowledging that you have a problem is powerful. This is the first step in the healing process. The second step to solving any problem is asking for help, which Elise and Robert did, and I honor and respect them so much for that. If you and your partner are experiencing financial challenges, the following is important to know:

1. Your struggles with money and personal finances are most likely the result of hardwired patterns that you learned in childhood, directly or indirectly, from your parents. These patterns are usually passed down from one generation to the next, which is why poverty remains the largest and most difficult condition in the world to overcome.
2. You were most likely not taught how to manage money or your personal finances in your home or at school, which left you (like most of the world's population) unprepared to make wise financial choices. It is very difficult for people to fully experience their personal and financial potential without this financial education as a foundation.
3. You may suffer from low financial self-esteem, which can lead to feelings of guilt and shame that can cause you to unconsciously self-sabotage. This can happen when we feel we've behaved "badly" and no longer believe that we deserve good things to happen.
4. These negative feelings and experiences form patterns in our brains, causing us essentially to "short-circuit" and become ineffective at managing our finances and making good decisions.

5. These patterns can be identified; and through awareness, actions, and support, you can begin to change these patterns and behaviors by learning new healthy ones over time.

Everyone (including you!) deserves help and a chance to make the changes necessary to create the life they truly want and deserve. Once you make a commitment to change and ask for help and support, you will have traveled a great distance. Next, you may need to get help from other professionals who can guide and support you to a new way of being.

Asking for Help

One of the most challenging things we humans grapple with is asking for help. It is as if we believe that asking for help is somehow a sign of weakness, when in fact it truly is the contrary. It is always a sign of strength and courage, never weakness. We must all work to overcome false pride that keeps us from reaching out for help or support when we need it, so that we don't waste precious time and energy, which are the most valuable resources any of us has or will ever have.

EXERCISE
Do We Need Help?

Answer these questions to help you determine if you need outside help:

1. Is there a persistent financial issue that causes you and your spouse to be in conflict regularly?

2. Do you or your spouse feel distant from the other due to this unresolved issue?
3. Does this or any other issue cause you to be financially secretive or protective with your partner?
4. Is this or a related issue preventing you from moving forward in other areas of your life?
5. Do you no longer feel financially safe in your relationship?

If you answered yes to at least three of the five questions above, you are clearly headed down the wrong path and could use help and support. Here's how to take ownership of the problem and approach your partner to get help:

"I have been doing a lot of soul-searching lately and feel like we're stuck in a problem (or circumstance) that we can't seem to solve on our own. I think we need help with (fill in the blank) and wonder if we might be able to talk and perhaps seek some outside help and support." (Note: If your partner is unwilling to get help with you, there is no reason why you shouldn't proceed to get help on your own. In many instances, I've observed that when one person seeks help and support and begins to make changes, the formerly reluctant partner, in seeing the positive results, often becomes more willing to participate.)

For Richer, for Poorer

As you are learning, our money issues often become triggered or magnified when financial pressures arise. Whether we are married or in a committed relationship, our money issues and patterns often collide and create conflict that can easily lead to disharmony with our mate.

I've been working with Joshua and Sue over the past year. Their marriage was seriously challenged when Joshua's business failed and he had difficulty finding new work; Sue felt let down, betrayed, and angry. They could barely speak to each other.

As we worked together, they began to understand each other's core money issues: Sue grew up in an alcoholic family, felt alone and abandoned, and had a deep need for stability. Joshua grew up feeling unsupported by his parents and felt largely alone throughout his childhood. As financial pressures mounted, they began to trigger each other's insecurities. As Sue became increasingly critical, demanding, and withholding of love and affection, Joshua shut down emotionally. Joshua's self-esteem was affected, and his efforts to find a job were unsuccessful. He repeatedly said that he felt like a loser. With some coaching, Joshua came to understand that some part of him believed he didn't deserve a family. In effect, both Sue's and Joshua's security and abandonment issues had become triggered under financial duress, and they unconsciously began to react from their childhood wounds.

This type of scenario is increasingly common as more and more couples experience job loss and mounting debts and increasingly have trouble making ends meet. Ultimately, this couple learned how to recognize their triggers and to see their circumstances for what they really were. Neither had any intention or desire to leave the relationship, so the fear of abandonment was not based on anything more than fear from the past. As they began to understand each other's fears, they were able to respond more compassionately and resolve their financial differences.

Living within Your Means

One of the most common money traps I see today happens when couples who are living beyond their means resist making cutbacks and changes in their lifestyle. I ask these clients to reflect on the questions "Do you own your lifestyle, or does your lifestyle own you? And how much money is enough?"

Invariably when I ask, "How much money is enough?" people throw out some random high number without really giving it much thought. Or sometimes people just freeze and say, "Gee, I don't know. I've never really thought about it." Few clients actually have a clear idea of how much enough is, which has led me to wonder: If we don't know how much is enough, what it looks or feels like, then how can we possibly begin to create it or recognize it when it arrives? If we can't imagine it, how can we possibly hope to create it? Now, take a moment to imagine the kind of world we could create if everyone had enough and could be satisfied and fulfilled with simply that: not too much, not too little, but just enough. Take a moment to journal on this concept.

EXERCISE
Determining Your "Enough"

Answer these questions in your money coaching journal:

1. How much money is enough for me?
2. What will it take to make me feel completely safe and content?
3. What does the concept of enough look and feel like for me? Describe this in detail.

Write a detailed vision for your life that includes what is most meaningful and essential to your sense of safety, security, and well-being. Approach this exercise from the perspective of a minimalist, just to try on the idea and see how it feels. I say this because, like many people, you may mistakenly believe that you "should" have more than it takes to feel truly happy and content. As long as we are driven by our internal or external shoulds, we risk becoming enslaved by our desires rather than satisfied by the fulfillment of our true needs and wants. When we can learn to be satisfied with "enough," anything beyond that simply becomes as icing on the cake. It may taste good, but the cake is sufficient and delicious unto itself.

As an example, here's what enough looks like to clients Joshua and Sue: "Our lives are filled with meaning and purpose. We have a home that is comfortable and easy to live in with lots of windows and light. We don't need a lot of things and seldom shop for things we don't need. We like to travel and prefer experiences to things. As long as we can have one travel adventure someplace new every year, we are easily content. We are both self-employed and know how to make money using our gifts and talents in a variety of ways. We may or may not ever retire (because there's too much left to do!), but planning for it is still important. Our daughter is married with children and lives nearby. We love being active grandparents and dote on our grandchildren as often as we can. Our home, family, and friends are among our life's greatest treasures."

Gratitude: The Antidote to Our Dissatisfaction

Gratitude is the best way of staying present with all that is good in your life, regardless of your financial circumstances. A daily gratitude practice can help to alleviate the pain of our circumstances. Sometimes, we can become so hyper-focused on our difficulties that we overlook the good things in our lives that are right in front of us. It is exactly during our most challenging times that we most need to remind ourselves of the blessings that exist in our lives right now. Meditation, prayer, and/or a gratitude practice can help sustain us and see us through our most difficult times.

Remember that your circumstances are not who you are but where you are. Never let your financial circumstances define you or your value and worth. In time, your financial challenges will shift, yet what you have now to be grateful for will remain, provided you've acknowledged and appreciated both the people and the things in your life for all that they are.

Here's what I invite you to do: Begin each day by making a list of ten things for which you are grateful. Carry this list with you, and whenever you feel anxious or stressed, refer to the list to remind you of the good and beauty that exist in your life.

Money, Meaning, and Value

Everyone feels vulnerable when it comes to money. It's a core survival issue that, when triggered, can make us feel fearful, anxious, sad, or angry. It's also an area of our lives that at times can feel out of control or deeply affected by the actions of others.

As we become more aware of our money patterns and behaviors, we can begin to make healthier choices. This is a great first step toward creating a new financial legacy for yourself and your relationship — a legacy built on self-awareness, knowledge, and power. But first we must each begin to understand and heal our relationship with money. What is money and its meaning in your life? Write about this in your journal and share it with your partner.

Money is a powerful energy force and medium of exchange. It is a tool and resource that we receive as a direct result of the actions and contributions that we put forth in the world. It flows in and out of our lives in direct relationship to our efforts and intentions. Whenever you feel fearful or anxious about money, spend time in reflection to determine what inside you needs attending to, and address those needs proactively. As you work together to understand and respect money, learn to enjoy its company in your lives and see how it allows you access to new experiences that you appreciate. But remember, money has nothing to do with who you are, nor does your bank balance increase or decrease your worth. Work toward creating a partnership of mutual respect with money, but never confuse your self-worth with your net worth.

EXERCISE

Determining Your True Value and Worth

Answer the following questions in your money coaching journal.

1. How do you actively and consciously value your partner?
2. What specific actions do you take to let your partner know you value him or her?
3. On what do you base your own and your partner's value and worth? Complete the sentences below to help you clarify this more fully.

    *   My personal value and worth is based on _____. (Make a list. Examples: my contribution to my family as a wife and mother, my value as a human being, the way I love and support others, my ideas, my creativity, my financial contributions to my home and community.)
    *   My partner's value and worth to me is based on _____. (Make a list. Examples: her contributions as a wife and life partner, her sense of humor, our shared interests, her love and nurturing of our children, her vision, her strength and honesty.)

One of the greatest money traps of all is to become so entangled in the material world that we forget our own true value and wealth, which are already within us. Each of us is intrinsically valuable and worthy, regardless of what we possess. I believe, as Oprah Winfrey said, that "worthiness is our birthright." What better time than now to claim yours together?

Chapter Seven

OVERCOMING FINANCIAL CHALLENGES AND SETBACKS

Ordinary riches can be stolen, real riches cannot.
In your soul are infinitely precious things
that cannot be taken from you.

— OSCAR WILDE, *The Soul of Man under Socialism*

When it comes to money, almost everyone has a story these days. Many of these stories are filled with financially challenging times, bad luck, loss, sadness, and anger. While I know that these stories are true and that real pain and hardship are associated with them, as a money coach I also know all too well the dangers of becoming trapped in your story. I have witnessed the disabling effect that it can have on one's life and family. Whether your relationship has been challenged by the economy, an illness, job loss, or just bad luck, I want you to know that your financial circumstances are not who you are. Even if you have lost your home or have gone bankrupt, these are merely your *financial circumstances*, which with time and effort will pass and improve. However, for that to happen, you must consciously choose to work together to move past any residual feelings of guilt, shame, anger, or resentment that have accumulated as a result of your experience.

Couples often hold on to their experiences and resentments far too long. If you find yourself in this situation, you will need to either find a way to pick up the pieces and move on, or hold on to your story like a broken trophy of the past that will define and diminish your life. I would recommend that, given the options, you find healthy ways to pick up the pieces and reassemble them into a new life — a life that is more financially balanced and aligned with your true values and needs. Allow your financial challenges to become the doorway for creating a new way of living that enriches, rather than depletes, your life. As you move forward to make the necessary changes to build this new life, know that change is a process that takes time, courage, faith, and commitment. It is not always easy, but it is *always* worth the journey.

Beware the Victim

In financially challenging times, the Victim archetype can easily arise in anyone's life. Unfortunately, the Victim often carries a self-fulfilling prophecy that is dark and destructive and can rob us of our life's energy and potential. Bad things can and do happen in our lives, but we must be watchful and vigilant in the presence of any Victim tendencies. During times of challenge, what we most need to do is call in the Warrior archetype, and become focused, determined, and proactive. Action is always the antidote to fear and to overcoming our financial challenges.

If you and your partner are experiencing financial challenges, I want you to know that regardless of what is happening, *you are free to choose a new life today*. No, it won't happen magically overnight, but you can create it together. The first step toward achieving this is to release the past. The past is over; it is no longer real. Today is all that we have. Period. Tomorrow represents hope and a promise. So, if there is only this moment and we are not present in it, we are *wasting it*. When we go backward into the painful events of the past, *we are choosing pain over presence*. If we project too far into the future and become frightened that we won't survive, we are choosing fear and projecting a painful and negative imagined reality into the future. This might be a good time to remember Newton's first law of motion: a thing in motion tends to stay in motion. In other words, what you focus on creates momentum in your life. At any given moment in time, we must realize the potential impacts we are creating by what we choose to focus on.

Tips for Couples in Financial Distress

It is not uncommon during times of financial challenge to experience relationship problems as well. If you are experiencing conflict in your relationship, here are some suggestions to help you through this time.

Stay Present and Calm

One of the best ways to manage any challenge is to meditate. Meditation not only calms down the nervous system but can actually change the physiology of your brain. While many people today do meditate, clients often tell me they have difficulty meditating when they're stressed about money. Here is a guided meditation process to help you and your partner to stay present and calm.

EXERCISE
Shower Meditation: Cleanse Your Fears Away

Start the water in your shower, and visualize yourself step-ping into a warm, healing waterfall. As you step into the water (literally), imagine yourself standing in the most beau-tiful, serene place on earth, immersed in healing waters. Simply stand and allow the water to run over you; feel the warm water soothing your body and spirit. Repeat this mantra: "I am cleansed of all anxiety and fear. I surren-der and release all negativity and judgment toward myself and all others. I am free, whole, complete, and ready to begin anew." Repeat this a few times before completing your shower. (Note: I recommend doing this in the shower because warm water relaxes the body, and water is both cleansing and healing for the body and spirit.)

Release the Past

Forgive yourself, your partner, and any others who have contrib-uted to your difficulties. Clear the slate and release the past. It is already history unless you pack it up and carry it with you every day, which can make moving forward like moving upstream in a river with a rock tied to each foot. In other words, it can make life very difficult!

Be Resourceful

Sometimes couples reach their breaking point and simply cannot or do not have the tools they need to rise above their circum-stances. If your relationship or your family is suffering because of financial challenges, and one or both of you are not coping well, seek outside help and support. You will find a list of resources at the back of this book. Regardless of your circumstances, you both deserve help, and your family is depending on you to take care of yourselves and your relationship.

Develop a Spiritual Practice

The role of the Magician in our life is to help us to recognize that we are never alone. The Magician holds the key to balance and transformation of whatever life brings us. The greatest answers and solutions to our life's challenges are always within us. When you take the time to pray or meditate, not only will you help yourself to stay calm and centered, but also you are allowing yourself to receive spiritual guidance and support. Take some time every day to commune with Spirit in whatever manner suits you. There is no greater source of comfort and support than giving yourself this time and space in which to heal and connect with the Source.

Here is a beautiful poem called "Prayer" by Charles Elkind to reflect on:

Pray for what you can not see.
Pray clearly
for what you can only faintly grasp.
Pray silently
from the core of your being.
Pray for healing.
Pray for humanity.

Pray lovingly
Pray deeply —
pray so deeply that
the prayer and the praying
become one.

How to Avoid Reactive Behaviors

Couples can become considerably more reactive under financial duress, so it's important to establish an agreement of how and when you talk about your financial issues. I recommend that you agree to do the following:

Support One Another

When you have financial challenges, you'll be more effective as a team. During hard times, couples need to be supportive and kind to one another. If one or both of you are leaking anger or resentment, it will affect you both, and your relationship will suffer. Use the new language tools offered in chapter 4 to learn how to communicate with care and compassion.

- Don't discuss money issues first thing in the morning or before going to bed. Morning money conversations can be a setup for a stressful day, and at night your bedroom should be a safe zone. Avoid discussing money or any other triggering subject before bedtime, as it may disturb your sleep. It's important to establish a specific time and place to talk about your money issues that honors both your and your partner's needs and schedules. Timing is everything! To prevent overwhelm, it is helpful to manage your financial issues one at a time. Here's what I suggest:

  1. Make a list of all your financial obligations.
  2. Order the list, starting with what needs to be managed first to prevent further challenges.
  3. Determine where you can make financial cutbacks.

4. Allocate your income to your financial priorities first. If you don't have enough money to cover all of your obligations, contact your creditors, explain your circumstances, and find out what your options are. If possible, ask for payment deferral or negotiate a payment plan.

• Don't go into avoidance. When you are fearful around money, the fight-or-flight response becomes activated and may cause you to want to run away from your problems. This will only make things worse, so now is the time to bring in your Warrior and stay proactive. Work as a team to stay engaged — divide and conquer! In doing so, you will feel better and be rewarded with progress, improved circumstances, and resolution.

Simple Strategies to Recover from Financial Setbacks

As you begin to reclaim your lives and recover from your financial circumstances, you may encounter unforeseen challenges or roadblocks to moving forward. Such challenges are not uncommon and are best managed calmly and proactively. Don't let yourselves become deterred. Engage the Warrior archetype and use the suggestions below to assist you in making progress one day at a time.

1. If you're heavily in debt and need help, contact American Consumer Credit Counseling, a nonprofit organization that can help you get back on track (www.consumer credit.com).
2. Contact the National Foundation for Credit Counseling and locate a certified credit counselor in your area to help

you (www.nfcc.org). It's important to work with people who are accredited in this arena, as there are lots of scams out there today.

3. Remember that another source of your financial issues may be unconscious money patterns and behavior acquired from childhood that you each brought into the relationship. Have compassion for yourself and your partner, and seek the help of a Certified Money Coach, accredited financial counselor, or therapist if your money patterns are creating larger issues than you can resolve on your own.

4. Most financial differences that couples have are due to a failure to effectively communicate their needs, fears, and grievances, which tend to accumulate over time. Learn to talk openly and calmly and without blame. If you have an unresolvable issue, seek professional guidance. Use the communication techniques outlined in chapter 4.

5. Find your way back to your true "needs and values." This will allow you and your partner to get back into alignment with your core values. It will also help you to create a lifestyle of simplicity and sustainability that most couples find highly rewarding.

Coping with Debt

It seems that almost everyone today is burdened by debt. According to a 2010 report of the Federal Reserve Bank, the average American family has about $15,799 in consumer debt alone. As a country, the United States has a total consumer debt of more than $2.43 trillion, and together we hold more than 600 million credit cards.

Remember, this process will be easier if you take on one

financial issue at a time. Otherwise, you can become emotionally triggered and overwhelmed. Spend thirty to sixty minutes a day managing your finances and debts to the best of your ability, and then put them away. Managing your debt and credit issues one day at a time will help you to make consistent progress. Just do the best you can.

Here are some other guidelines for managing debt issues in your relationship:

1. Understand that you are not your debt. Your debt represents where you are financially, not who you are.
2. Make a commitment to understanding your spending patterns so that you can form a new awareness of your shopping habits and impulses. Keep a small notebook to record both your daily purchases and your mood or emotions at the time of purchase. Notice if you tend to shop or buy impulsively for emotional reasons.
3. If you have any feelings of guilt or shame associated with being in debt, work on forgiving yourself (or your partner) and release the past. The past is history, and you can choose to do it differently moving forward.
4. Find ways to cut back and simplify your life personally and financially. What do you truly need to be happy and feel secure? Write this down in your money journal.
5. Make a spending plan that includes both saving and debt repayment to the best of your financial ability. Even little efforts will make a difference and will increase your self-esteem. Use the Summary of Monthly Cash Flow — Spending Plan (see next page) as a tool for gaining clarity about your income and expenses.

Summary of Monthly Cash Flow — Spending Plan

Summary of Monthly Income (Inflow)

Salary, wages	$_____
Other business income	$_____
Interest income	$_____
Other	$_____
Total monthly income	$_____

Summary of Monthly Personal Expenses (Outflow)

Mortgage, rent	$_____
Loans	$_____
Credit cards	$_____
Taxes	$_____
Phone	$_____
Utilities	$_____
Food/groceries	$_____
Clothing	$_____
Laundry/cleaning	$_____
Personal care	$_____
Child care	$_____
Education	$_____
Medical insurance/care	$_____
Cable	$_____
Car payment	$_____
Car insurance	$_____
Gasoline	$_____
Car maintenance	$_____
Housekeeping	$_____
Entertainment	$_____
Vacation/travel	$_____
Gifts	$_____
Charitable giving	$_____
Miscellaneous	$_____
Total monthly personal expenses	$_____

Summary of Monthly Cash Flow — Spending Plan

Summary of Monthly Business Expenses (Outflow)

Advertising	$_____
Accounting	$_____
Taxes	$_____
Phone	$_____
Utilities	$_____
Education	$_____
Insurance	$_____
Auto	$_____
Travel	$_____
Meals	$_____
Professional fees	$_____
Supplies	$_____
Postage	$_____
IRA/SEP-IRA	$_____
Books and publications	$_____
Services	$_____
1099 — employees	$_____
Payroll and salaries	$_____
Total monthly business expenses	**$_____**

Totals

Total monthly inflow	$_____
Total monthly outflow (Total monthly personal expenses + total monthly business expenses	− $_____
Total monthly net flow	$_____

Your net flow is your bottom line (that is, discretionary income).

6. If your debt load is overwhelming and preventing you from sleeping or living a normal life, seek the help of a certified debt or credit counselor. Remember, you deserve help and support, so reach out for assistance.

7. Debt can be a source of major stress, so integrate stress management techniques into your daily life and nurture yourself by exercising, eating well, and committing to a daily spiritual practice.

8. If you are feeling deeply depressed, paralyzed, or unable to cope with your financial circumstances, seek the help of a therapist or social worker.

9. If you know deep down that you cannot afford to pay your debts and it's hurting your health, family, or life, seek the advice of an attorney and consider bankruptcy as an option. Ultimately, bankruptcy is about financial forgiveness and giving people a second chance, which everyone deserves. Know that your life, health, and family are far more important than any debts you may owe.

Coping with Credit Issues

Couples often find it difficult to move forward financially due to mistakes they have made in the past. Some of these mistakes have negatively impacted their credit or even their ability to get proper housing or a job, which is truly sad and unfortunate. Access to housing should be a constitutional right that can never be denied anyone due to credit history or financial mistakes. Nothing should infringe upon this. However, not everyone believes accordingly, and today, many couples and their families are having difficulty getting housing or even getting a job due to their credit history. If your relationship is challenged by these circumstances, here are some steps you can take:

1. Begin with forgiveness, which is the most spiritually correct action we can ever take. Together, as you begin to heal on the *inside*, know that you are also clearing the space for manifesting something new on the *outside*.

2. Write a letter (to be given to a potential employer or landlord) and explain your circumstances to them up front so that there is no surprise. Tell them everything you have done in your life to make amends for the past and to improve your life. Let them know who you are today.

3. Get two or three letters of reference from people who can attest to the changes you've made (preferably not relatives), such as your pastor, a friend, or a former employer.

4. Include your personal letter and these reference letters with your application. Tell the potential employer or landlord that you would greatly appreciate a second chance. Let them know that you are a good person who will do everything in your power to be worthy of that chance.

   In general, people are more willing to help you if you're straight with them in the beginning and make an effort to help them to see who you really are. Otherwise, all they have to work with is your credit score and/or your legal record, which is not at all who you are.

Coping with Job Loss and Unemployment

Being unemployed can be scary and challenging, personally and financially. Hanging in there, interview after interview, requires great faith and fortitude, and the greatest danger that I have witnessed in my clients is the loss of confidence or hope. Here are some of the actions I've recommended that my clients have found helpful:

- Avoid negativity. Take a break from negative news and media. Even though the job market is tight, many companies are still hiring.
- Reconnect with family members, friends, and former business associates; they may know of possible opportunities.
- Review your skills, talents, and abilities. Perhaps you have skills that you've forgotten or that can be applied in a different way or field than you thought possible.
- Pay attention to how you are spending your time — it's your most valuable asset! Be proactive in your job search every day.
- Get support from a coach or career counselor if you need it — you don't have to go it alone!
- Create consistent self-care habits that will help you to stay healthy and positive. Eat well, exercise, take walks, pray, meditate, get plenty of sleep, and avoid excessive use of caffeine and alcohol.
- Stay connected to friends and family for support and encouragement.
- Keep your eyes and ears open — opportunities can present themselves in unexpected ways and places.
- Make at least five phone calls daily to people you know who have jobs and find out if their company has any positions open that might be suitable for you.
- Don't isolate yourself — get out of the house every day and explore the job options in your own community. Don't just spend your time on the Internet, sending out countless résumés. Get nicely dressed and hand-deliver your résumé to companies.

EXERCISE
Visualization

1. With your eyes closed, picture yourself in an interview for a job that you know you would like.
2. Picture yourself shaking the interviewer's hand as he or she offers you a position.
3. Picture yourself working in an environment that you know you would enjoy. Hold this image for a few minutes while taking deep, relaxing breaths.
4. Now go about your day, and whenever you feel fearful about not finding a job, repeat this visualization and hold it as your template and intention for receiving a new job.

Rebuilding Your Self-Esteem

Whether unemployed or just struggling financially, people who are experiencing financial challenges often suffer a loss of self-esteem. When this happens, they can lose confidence and become disconnected from their talents and gifts. This can present a problem, as you need to be connected to your skills and strengths in order to present well in an interview with a potential employer.

EXERCISE
Life Inventory Process

This exercise will help you to build your self-esteem and connect you to your skills, talents, and abilities. It's called the Life Inventory Process, and it's designed to help you to become clear about your unique offering.

Doing this exercise will allow you to gain clarity about

all that you have to offer a potential employer, which, unfortunately, is seldom completely covered in a simple résumé. The Life Inventory Process is a good way to address this issue so that you're prepared when you get an interview. Here's how it works:

1. Make a list of your life's *highlights and achievements*, from elementary school to the present. Include areas of your life where you shined when you were a child, such as sports, art, or schoolwork. Even little successes count. The purpose of this exercise is to help you to reconnect with aspects of yourself that you may have forgotten by helping you to recall the achievements in your life.

   When you are done, hang up this list somewhere in your home as a reminder of what you've done well in your life and to boost your self-esteem. (Note: This is a self-esteem-building exercise, so don't give the list to a potential employer. But you can take it with you to the interview as a reminder of all that you have to offer.)

2. Now make a list of your *personal assets*, which should include all the skills, talents, and abilities you've acquired during your lifetime through education, life experience, and work experience. These personal assets are your gifts, and they are an integral part of who you are. You own these gifts outright, and the knowledge of them can never be taken from you. Now, review your list to see if there are possible moneymaking opportunities that you've overlooked. Ask yourself what other options might utilize some of your experience and gifts.

Here's an affirmation for today: I fully own my skills and strengths. I have much to offer a potential employer. My perfect job and employer are being created for me now. I see them, I know them, and it is so.

Monitoring Your Thoughts

When we are challenged, personally and financially, it can be difficult to stay centered, calm, and positively proactive. Yet, if we can't make these necessary adjustments, our lives can spiral downward into negativity and defeat. One of the things I teach my clients is to actively listen to and guard their thoughts vigilantly. Negative thoughts are like thieves that enter in the night and rob you of your higher good and potential. Here's an exercise that can help you to stay focused and positive. This is especially critical when you are trying to recover from a financial setback or need to find a new job, if you're unemployed.

EXERCISE
Mind Watch

Find a quiet place to sit comfortably for ten minutes a day. Gently inform your mind that you are present and on watch.

As you sit, notice how your mind drifts from one thought to another. Whenever you notice a negative thought, calmly repeat these words: "Access denied...cancel thought." There is nothing else for you to do. Do not let these negative thoughts disturb your peace. They do not have any power over you unless you allow them access to your mind.

This process is a gentle form of training your mind. It can help you learn how to control your thoughts rather than being controlled by them. If you commit to doing this process consistently, you will begin to notice your thoughts *all the time* and ultimately learn to automatically "deny access" and "cancel" any negative or counterproductive thoughts as they arise. This exercise is highly effective for maintaining good mental hygiene. I call it mental floss, and it's good to do daily to prevent thought decay!

No matter what financial hardships you may be undergoing, it is very important for you to acknowledge that you and your gifts are valuable. When you value and express your gifts freely and without attachment to a monetary outcome, you will feel better about yourself and feel more energized and enlivened. Then, with this renewed energy, you can move forward to focus on revitalizing your career and improving your financial circumstances. Perhaps, along the way, someone may hire you to do what you love. If not, it's still a blessing to have a job that supports you and your family while you continue to express your gifts, whenever and however you can.

Thirty-Day Fast from Fear: A New Diet for Humanity

The following is a fasting from fear program that I developed to help my clients detox from the internal poisons we accumulate due to a steady diet of fear, anxiety, and stress. This diet can help spiritually inoculate you and your partner from any residual negativity or darkness created by your circumstances. Fear simply breeds more fear and does not produce anything positive or life affirming. Fear is the enemy, but one that we can defeat through our commitment to daily right action.

We are living in one of the most interesting and turbulent times ever in the history of the world. Yes, I know it feels uncomfortable, but we have great power and potential within us, and we can and must be resourceful and resilient.

I invite you to participate in this Thirty-Day Fast from Fear Program. It will help you to stay positive, grounded, and connected to God. It can't hurt, and it may just help you to create a whole new way of living your life.

Follow these steps every day for thirty days — it'll take less than ten minutes a day!

PRAY UPON RISING. *Thank you for this day and for the rich opportunities this day will bring. I pray for your love and light to guide me in all my endeavors, that I am safe, that I am protected, that I am free to express my gifts, that I may have work that fulfills me and nourishes my life, personally and financially. I am eternally grateful for all that is and have complete faith and trust that all my needs are met. And so it is. Amen.*

MEDITATE. Use the guided shower meditation offered earlier in this chapter, or simply sit calmly and quietly in bed for ten to twenty minutes each morning.

USE AN AFFIRMATION. Repeat this affirmation before you leave your home each day: *I surrender fear and choose to be guided by faith in all my actions and choices today.*

DO A REALITY CHECK. Whenever feelings of fear or negativity arise, ask yourself if there is any real or present danger to your well-being. If not, then know that any fear you may be feeling is simply a projection (like a movie), because no real danger exists. Remind yourself that F.E.A.R. means "False Evidence Appearing Real" (as written by Unity founder Charles Fillmore). Write this on a sticky note: "F.E.A.R. means False Evidence Appearing Real." Place it on your computer at work, your bathroom mirror, or someplace highly visible as a constant reminder.

PRACTICE GRATITUDE DAILY. Every day, focus on one thing you have to be grateful for, and keep your attention focused on gratitude for this throughout the day. *Today I am grateful for* _____.

KEEP A FEAR-BUSTER JOURNAL. At the end of each day, write down any fearful, fretful, angry, or negative thoughts that have come up. Get these thoughts outside of your mind and energetic space. Thoughts do matter! Do not house negative or fearful thoughts inside you — move them out in healthy ways.

PRACTICE GENEROSITY. Challenge yourself to do one generous thing for someone else every day. Open a door, carry someone's groceries, offer to babysit for a friend, call your mother and tell her how much she has given you, tell your child how much you appreciate who they are and what they bring to your life, take your dog for a walk. Generosity comes in many forms and is always life affirming.

Chapter Eight

NEGOTIATING MONEY CONFLICTS AND DIFFERENCES

Out beyond ideas of wrongdoing and right-doing,
there is a field. I'll meet you there.

— RUMI, *The Big Red Book*

Throughout this book, I've provided exercises and tools to help you understand your individual and relationship money patterns, build healthy communication skills, and better navigate the money domain in your lives. Hopefully, you've been doing the exercises together and are growing more financially aware and intimate by the day. Now it is time to take your skills a bit deeper as you learn how to negotiate any financial conflicts or differences that exist now or may arise in the future.

It is common for couples to have differences in their values, beliefs, and behaviors relative to money, and frequently these differences are the root cause of many of our relationship issues. Sometimes couples come to see me because they need someone objective to help them resolve their financial differences, especially those involving children, debt, inheritance issues, or large financial commitments. I recently worked with a couple, Jessica and Max, who were happily married until Max inherited a large sum of money from his father, who had passed away suddenly. His father's trust stipulated that the funds in the trust could pass only to *their children* in the event that Max died and made no mention of Jessica.

While this type of control from the grave is not uncommon, it can and does create conflict in many relationships. In this case, it was particularly sensitive for Jessica because she knew that her father-in-law had always disapproved of her and felt that she wasn't good enough for Max. While polite, he had always been cold and indifferent to her. Now, Max suddenly had great wealth, as would her children someday, and Jessica felt completely disregarded. As Max began to push to make some major financial decisions, including the purchase of a new home, Jessica increasingly felt like an outsider and would tell him, "It's your money — do whatever you want." As I worked with them, Jessica was able to see how her fears and insecurities from her childhood had become triggered and had resurfaced. Raised by a single mother who often left her alone while she worked or partied, Jessica often went unfed and felt scared and abandoned by her mother. Suddenly, she had become that frightened little girl again.

Through our work together, Max learned that he needed to step up and assure Jessica that he would take care of her and never abandon her as her mother had. He set up a life insurance trust to address her financial needs in the event of his death. They learned how to work as a team in a new way that allowed their new wealth to enhance their life rather than create separation and distance. Max learned that if he wanted Jessica to become a part of their financial decisions, he needed to not only include her in the financial decision-making process but also empower her to become his financial partner. Today, their marriage is stronger than ever before.

Many of the conflicts and issues that couples encounter are not rational and may even, on the surface, seem completely illogical. This is largely due to those hardwired emotional patterns stored in our brain that, when triggered, cause us to become reactive. However, as long as one person commits to staying calm and present in the middle of these reactive behaviors, your conflicts will be less likely to spiral out of control.

Clarifying and Aligning Your Values

Many of the financial differences and conflicts about money that couples experience stem from a clash in values, and the key to negotiating your financial differences is to first understand and clarify your values. Becoming aligned in your values can greatly facilitate your ability as a couple to honor and manage your differences. Frequently, couples come from very different socioeconomic backgrounds, which can greatly influence and inform their money patterns and behaviors. Such was the case for a couple I worked with, Sara and Elijah. Sara was an only child who came from a wealthy family. Elijah was raised in a middle-class family, and his parents were both blue-collar workers. His family worked hard, saved whatever they could, and were very frugal. Sara's family, on the other hand, came from a long line of inherited wealth, and she seldom ever heard the word *no*. Both Sara and Elijah were well-educated professionals, but their values, especially regarding money, were extremely different.

They had a prenuptial agreement (which is quite common for those with inherited wealth), so they kept and managed their money separately, except for the expenses they had in common, such as their home. Elijah was more than content with a rather simple life and was quite frugal. Sara enjoyed the finer things in life and spent lavishly on their home, her clothes, art, jewelry, dining out, and expensive vacations. These differences were challenging for Elijah because not only could he not afford to keep up with his wife's expensive tastes, but also he didn't want to, and he believed that Sara spent her money foolishly and wastefully. His disapproval of Sara increased over time, and she began to feel judged and criticized. By the time they came to see me, their differences had formed a wedge between them and they had reached a crisis point.

Even in our first session together, it was apparent to me that Elijah and Sara were experiencing a values clash in their relationship. What wasn't so apparent at first was *why* these differences had grown into a full-blown conflict. The first thing I had Elijah and Sara do was address their values. As we explored this, they discovered considerable differences.

The greatest difference and primary conflict was about money: Sara had always been able to have and experience the things she was natively drawn to, such as art, design, beauty, and creativity. She is a Creator/Artist archetype to her core. Elijah, on the other hand, is a lover of nature and an environmentalist whose core values clash with his wife's lavish lifestyle. In addition, Elijah is simply more financially frugal and conservative, while Sara has never even had to think about saving or being frugal. She has a trust fund in addition to her earnings, and she can easily afford to spend as she does. Neither Elijah nor Sara is wrong for what they value; they are just different. Left unmanaged, however, their differences would surely have eroded their intimacy and respect, and ultimately destroyed their relationship.

I worked with Sara and Elijah for about two months, helping

them to identify and understand each other's core money patterns and behaviors and the influence of their primary money types on their relationship. One of the most amazing things they discovered through this process was that Elijah had an unconscious pattern and belief (inherited from his family) that rich people were greedy and bad, which, of course, is not only untrue but completely irrational (although sadly, may people hold this belief). Unconsciously, this belief worked away at Elijah like a wound that would not heal. Sara's spending and financial choices were like salt in his wound, causing him to become agitated and critical, which only made Sara retreat into even more spending (an inherited pattern she learned from her mother — if it hurts, go shopping). As Sara and Elijah came to understand the underlying beliefs and behaviors that were causing their disconnection, they grew more compassionate and loving again. We worked together to create new agreements that incorporated their shared needs and values.

EXERCISE
Values

Complete the exercise below in your individual money coaching journals. Once you've both finished the exercise, share your responses and discuss the exercise together.

1. To determine your shared values and differences, you'll each make a list of your personal values. Your values represent what is important to you and underlie your core beliefs.
2. Once you've completed your lists, circle the values that you share and create a shared-values list. Acknowledge and honor what you both value.

3. Discuss ways in which you can better bridge the gap between your differences by focusing on and strengthening your shared values.

For example, since the environment was so important to Elijah, Sara agreed to recycle more and try as much as possible to buy items that were more environmentally friendly. In addition, they agreed to take more eco-friendly vacations together. Sara even traded in her luxury car for a hybrid, and Elijah was thrilled and touched by her gesture. They recently decided to start a family and have agreed to work together as a team, committing themselves to staying on the same page when it comes to raising their children to be financially aware and mindful.

Healing through Narrative

Narrative writing as a way of speaking our truth has been used throughout time. I find it very useful as a way for couples to explore each other's perspectives in a nonthreatening manner. Here are money narratives written by Sara and Elijah; the process was cathartic and healing for them both.

Sara's Narrative

"From the moment I first met Elijah, I felt that I'd found my home. He was so honest, open, and transparent. I didn't feel like I had to protect myself or hide any part of who I was. Given my family dynamics and money, I have been taught to be cautious and suspicious of men and have been used by others in the past. Elijah never seemed interested in money; in fact, he was so down-to-earth that it felt as if money didn't matter to him at all. I know he felt a bit awkward with my family's wealth, but he never let them intimidate him or make him feel less than, which they certainly know how to do! He has always known who he is and is so comfortable in his own skin. All I've ever known about myself is that I'm a person of privilege and wealth that isn't even mine, which comes with a fair amount of emotional baggage. I've tried the best I could to be worthy of the wealth I've been given, but sometimes I still feel guilty and separate from others. Elijah changed this for me. Money was *never* what we were about. Our love was based upon connection, attraction, and common interests, and I've always felt at ease and at peace with him. Until all that ended, and my money and wealth became the elephant in the room. Now I feel his eyes watching me with disdain. I see his contempt every time I bring something home, like a painting I've fallen in love with, and his questions lash out at me as judgments. 'Did you really need one more painting? Do you know how many people you could have fed with that money?' And lately, I notice that shopping has become a refuge for me just like it was for my mother, who shopped to escape my father's extramarital affairs. I know that I'm spoiled, but I'm not a bad person. I love and miss Elijah and who we used to be."

Elijah's Narrative

"Sara lit up the room when she walked into it. She has so much grace and class; you can't help but look at her. But deep down she's sweet, sensitive, and vulnerable, and all I ever wanted was to love and protect her from the world. She's the most creative person I know, and her taste and love of beauty are truly magical. Her family's wealth was daunting at first, as my parents sometimes barely made ends meet. I decided that I could never be with Sara unless I could get beyond her wealth and I loved her enough to not let it be an issue. But after we married, Sara seemed to be obsessed with creating the perfect home, the perfect life, and everything we owned had to be the best and most expensive. At first, this was kind of fun, but after a few years, it began to wear on me. All this stuff, fancy parties, fancy friends...it just feels wasteful and inauthentic to me. I see the world around me suffering, people in poverty, the environment being destroyed, and feel like all this greed and consumption is the cause of it. It makes me feel sick to my stomach. I do very much love my wife, but I don't like this lifestyle, and I feel like a stranger in my own home. I long for a simpler, more connected relationship with my wife."

Writing Your Money Narrative

Your money narrative is different from your money story, which we covered in chapter 2. Your money story represents the history of money in your life, from early childhood to present. Your money narrative is told in the first person and describes your feelings and experience about money and your relationship together from the beginning to the present day. Write your narrative as though you were telling this story to a third party and wanted them to understand your dilemma or perspective. If you feel comfortable and safe, read your money narratives out loud to each other and discuss them openly. Thank each other for sharing and perhaps do the Ho'oponopono exercise provided in chapter 4.

Ground Rules for Resolving Financial Differences

Money conflicts are inevitable in every relationship. How you choose to deal with them when they do arise can make all the difference in the world. When conflicts occur, you can resolve them quickly by using the following steps:

- Connect with your heart.
- Calmly express your needs, wants, and concerns openly without criticism or blame.
- Clearly state your need or request.
- No yelling or name-calling. If this begins, take a time-out.
- No interrupting each other. Take turns speaking for up to five minutes at a time without interruption.
- Listen and respond.
- If you need time to think or process your feelings, say so, and then come back together in an hour or so. Don't wait too long, or your partner will feel ignored or invalidated.
- Finally, discuss and make a new agreement as to how you can resolve your conflict or difference.

Spend Some, Save Some, Give Some Away

Years ago, I had a client in her seventies who was widowed and had grown up during the Depression. She lived simply and frugally, yet she was one of the happiest, most contented people I have ever met. She never used credit cards, her house was paid off, she had plenty of savings, and in her retirement, her one big luxury was to go out to dinner once a week. She loved good food, and so we dined together occasionally. Once, during a dinner conversation, I asked her if she would share her secret to being so financially wise and content; this is what she said:

My husband and I were so happy that we found each other that it didn't matter what we had or did as long as we had each other. We had a little accounting business, and our philosophy was simple, but it worked well for us. This is what it was: *Every check you get, you should spend some, save some, and give some away.* We lived like that quite happily for over fifty years!

What she and her husband had mastered is something I see very few people able to do: they lived within their means.

Since most of us are not properly educated about how to make wise financial choices, it can be challenging to know what the right decision is for ourselves and our relationships. We tend to be driven by our desires and impulses rather than by wisdom and logic. To help couples to make wise financial decisions, I came up with a little formula. Try following these steps the next time you have a financial decision that you need to make together:

1. Ask yourselves, do we really need it or just want it?
2. If you really need it, begin to evaluate your options.
3. If you simply want it, ask yourselves if the purchase will create any unnecessary stress or consequences in your life or strain in your relationship. If not and you can afford it, proceed to the next step.
4. Determine what you can afford, and then stick to your budget.
5. Do some research on the product or service before going to make the purchase.
6. Compare options and pricing.
7. If you're torn between two choices, make a list of the pros and cons of each (the longest pro list wins).
8. If the choices are close, choose the one you *both* like the best.
9. If you feel uncertain or confused, ask for guidance and support.

10. Don't let anyone pressure you into a decision before you're both ready and feel confident in your choice. If the decision is causing a serious conflict, don't move forward until you both agree. When you cannot agree and don't work together to make important financial decisions, you are essentially devaluing your relationship in favor of *something* rather than the *someone* who loves you and keeps you warm at night. Nothing you own will ever be able to provide that for you.

11. Every time you go out alone to purchase something, stop and check in with your true feelings, and ask yourself these important questions:

    - Why do I want this? What need does buying this fulfill?
    - Is there something else I can do or ask for (without spending money) to take care of my needs?
    - Will it give me greater peace to spend this money, save it, or give it away?

If you do this process regularly, it will slow down your decision-making process considerably, which will allow you to make clearer, more informed financial choices. As you begin to make better choices around money, not only will you increase your self-esteem, but also you'll learn to trust each other more, which is the foundation of all intimacy. As this occurs, your capacity for receiving greater abundance and prosperity will grow as well. Working together to resolve the financial differences in your relationship is definitely a sign of strength and commitment. In many cases, I have found that money issues in relationships are a *symptom* of another problem that is not being managed or perhaps even fully recognized. For example, if your wife has been feeling scared and worn down by life and financial circumstances and doesn't feel you are doing enough or the right actions to improve your circumstances, then the real issue to address may be her feelings of fear, disappointment, or distrust.

Accepting and Honoring Your Differences

Partners seldom fully recognize or acknowledge how their differences are, or at least can be, a wonderful advantage. Without realizing it, we can become stuck and inflexible in our opinions and fail to see how our differences actually help to balance us out, expanding our thinking and thus our perspective of ourselves and the world around us. If you always agreed with your partner on everything, one of you would be unnecessary to the mix. When it comes to our love relationships, sometimes we need a worthy opponent who helps us to see another point of view that perhaps we were blind to or afraid of seeing. When you can honor and accept your differences for what they bring into your life and how they cause you to grow and expand beyond your limited thinking or ways of being, your differences become a blessing.

EXERCISE

Honoring Your Differences

Try this exercise to begin to identify the advantages of your differences.

1. Each of you make a list of all the ways you feel that you are *different* from each other (in general, as well as with regard to money).

2. Circle the words or differences that challenge you the most about your partner.
3. In what ways have these aspects of your partner caused you to grow or change as a person?
4. Take turns acknowledging and honoring your differences and how they have helped you to grow or expand as a person and as a couple.

Chapter Nine

KIDS AND MONEY

Children will not remember you for the material things
you provided but for the feeling that you cherished them.

— RICHARD L. EVANS

By now you have probably observed how your own
money patterns and behaviors have influenced the way you parent your children with respect to money. Most parents unconsciously pass down their patterns and beliefs to their children,
which is why these behaviors tend to be multigenerational and
deeply entrenched. That is, until one by one we begin doing our
own work, recognize the patterns, and decide to break the cycle
and commit to leaving our children a more financially empowered
legacy. So how do we, as loving parents, do this? Consciously,
carefully, and one step at a time.

One of the greatest challenges I've observed in relationships
is when parents bring their own unconscious money issues into

their parenting. I've witnessed many parents trying (unsuccessfully) to resolve their own childhood money wounds through their children, which can lead to conflicts over child rearing. Here are some of the most common differences that I've seen and worked with:

- Overgiving to children, especially on birthdays and holidays
- Overcompensating for feelings of guilt or inadequacies with money or gifts
- Using money as a form of control or to manipulate children
- Involving children in money disputes with ex-spouses
- Giving money as a way to placate a child
- Giving money instead of love, time, or attention
- Allowing children to play off of you or your spouse's money differences (for example, you're generous, your spouse is frugal, and when he says no, the child moves on to you to get a more desired result; this is a big "no-no")
- Fighting about money in the presence of children

Any of the issues above can become a source of conflict in a relationship or marriage. But the bottom line is, these behaviors are truly potentially harmful to your children as well as your relationship. Of greatest concern to me is fighting about money in front of your kids. I cannot tell you how many adults I've worked with who developed both money fears and money aversion due to witnessing their parents' fights around money. Fights are frightening to children and can cause them to develop fearful and reactive patterns. This can also happen when parents going through a divorce put their child in the middle of their money disputes.

Many of my clients have tremendous money issues caused by having to be the one to beg their father for the alimony check and bear whatever wrath that might have entailed. In the new field of financial therapy, this is referred to as *financial incest*, as it is inappropriate and forces a child to engage in adult financial matters.

Compensatory Love

Another major issue is something I call *compensatory love*, which is usually an inherited pattern from childhood. Compensatory love is when one or both parents give money or gifts as compensation for something they feel guilty about (such as working too much) or as a substitute for something they aren't comfortable giving, such as closeness or affection. Unfortunately, this is confusing to a child and can cause him or her to grow up believing that money and things are love, which they are most certainly not. If you have children, you owe it to them and to yourself to heal your childhood money wounds so as not to inflict them on your kids.

Getting on the Same Page

Parents (and stepparents) need to get on the same page and set a good, clear, and consistent example about money early in their children's lives. Here are four steps that will help this to happen:

1. Begin to identify and understand your own money patterns and behaviors (doing the exercises in the other chapters in this book is a good place to start!) so that you don't unconsciously pass the negative or challenging patterns down to your children.

2. Sit down together and calmly discuss how to raise your children to be financially aware and empowered.
3. Clear up and negotiate any differences you might have.
4. Create new agreements, and then keep and model them well in your lives together.

I also highly recommend that you agree to the following money tactics:

- Give more love and time than you do money or gifts. You can never love a child too much, but you can overgive things and money to the point where your child begins to think these things are love.
- If one of you says no to something, it's a firm no. Children are famous for triangulating their parents, and this is not a healthy way to parent. If your child attempts this behavior, clearly and firmly let him or her know that the behavior will not be tolerated. Agree to never veto each other's decisions. If you really disagree, discuss this privately and not in front of the children. Never use money or gifts as a means of manipulating or placating your child. This will eventually backfire, as children are smart and can quickly figure out how to manipulate you as well.

Allowance or Not?

While not all experts agree on this subject, I strongly believe that if you choose to give your children an allowance, they should be required to earn it by doing *something*, provided that they are old enough. This establishes a good work ethic and shared responsibility in creating a home life. Teaching your children to be empowered to help out at an early age is important. Starting at about age six or seven, most children are capable of handling simple tasks and responsibilities around the house. This not only helps them to learn important and necessary life skills but also greatly increases their self-esteem and makes them feel *capable*. When we do everything for our kids and don't allow them to participate in our lives or share in the responsibilities of family life, we're actually cheating them.

One of the greatest gifts you can ever give your child is a sense of their own *capacity*. While it is great to be a loving parent who caters to your child's needs, too much caretaking can actually cause a child to feel *incapable* of doing things on their own and make the world seem too big or scary. Of course, you will always need to match the task and responsibility with what is appropriate for the child's age. Give them tasks that are safe and that they can succeed at. Our children really enjoy being given responsibility (even if they balk!). It gives them a sense of achievement and makes them feel good about themselves.

Steps to Raising Financially Empowered Children

One of the most important things we can do to foster a healthy relationship with our children is to talk with them about money in a healthy and consistent manner. When you have calm, open conversations about money with your family on a fairly regular basis, you normalize the subject of money and move it beyond the taboo.

It is also important to be honest and direct with our children. Children are very sensitive, and they feel what's going on even if you're not telling them. When you are having money problems, it is best to engage in candid but careful money conversation with your kids. For example, if you have children under the age of eight, after dinner is over, tell them you want to talk to them about money. Gently tell them that due to the economy (or job loss or whatever), you might not have as much money for a while, and you will all need to work together as a family to make some changes. Then tell them what sacrifices might need to be made (no more cable, video games, private lessons, and so on). If they react, let them know that this doesn't mean forever, but it is necessary right now. Then reassure them that they are safe, you will always take care of them, and they don't need to worry because as their parents, you'll figure it out. As long as you're all together, you have everything you need. You might also explain that many families have the same issues so that they know your family is not alone in this. Keep it light, and let them know that you can still have a lot of fun just hanging out more as a family, playing games and doing things that don't cost money, like camping and hiking, which can bring you closer together.

Honoring Your Differences

Disputes over children and money are common in relationships. Parenting styles vary, and sometimes one person feels it's okay to spoil a child by giving them everything they want, while the other believes the money would be better spent on a college fund. It is best to agree on these things before you have kids, but if you already have children, you might want to find a way to honor both sides. Set up a "fun fund" and a college fund, allocating resources to both reasonably and within your budget. This is respectful of your differences and is better for the children in the long run.

College-Age Kids and Young Adults

How can we better support our youth in the face of a constantly shifting economy? As parents and elders, we can provide mentoring, opportunities, and encouragement to help college students and young adults to become financially empowered. It saddens me to see so many young people who feel lost and overwhelmed by debt or who are having difficulty finding decent-paying work. Where money is concerned, offer them guidance and support in creating a monthly budget and planning for unexpected expenses and their future. Most of all, encourage them to avoid getting into unnecessary credit card debt, a trend that sadly is becoming an epidemic among college students and young adults. Don't assume that your kids know how to do this on their own or that they have learned these critical life skills at school, as this is rarely the case.

If you are the parents of a young adult, it is important for you to maintain the broader vision for your kids and to remember that their world is very different from the one we encountered at their age. Undoubtedly, young entrepreneurship is one of the megatrends that will continue to expand over the years to come. It makes good sense for a young person to learn the skills of self-sufficiency, innovation, and practical business sense that are required to successfully launch and manage a business. As technology and the Internet continue to expand in new ways like social networking, Generation Y'ers, who are hardwired for technology, may very well be the generation most suited to harness these technologies in ways we haven't yet imagined. With our encouragement and support, these revolutionary tools could easily begin to create new career opportunities. So, encourage and support the young adults in your life to believe in themselves, and help them to hold a longer-term vision of growth and possibility for their lives and the world around them. They greatly need your help and support in finding their way. After all, the future of the world depends on them.

Adult Children

We are living in the age of the "boomerang generation," when for both economic and personal reasons, many adult children leave home only to keep bouncing back. Or sometimes, as the movie *Failure to Launch* demonstrated so well, one or both parents can't stop caretaking their grown children. This is most common with Martyr archetypes and can cause serious challenges in the relationship if one partner is not in agreement with financially supporting grown children. I have had many parents in their sixties and seventies call me and beg me to help their child become a self-sustaining adult. This is generally my response: there is usually a reason why your adult child isn't financially making it out there in the real world, and it may be you.

In my experience, the patterns around this begin early and can be hard to break unless the parents set some clear boundaries. Most often, these failure-to-launch issues are due to deep-seated fears and insecurities, which may require therapy in addition to coaching. Although it can be tough, sometimes we have to surrender our kids to Spirit and let them take a shot at doing it on their own, even if they fail. Besides, failure is nothing more than research that teaches us what does not work. These lessons can be strong medicine for those who are reluctant to grow up. On the other hand, if you have an adult child who is emotionally or mentally unstable, they may be unable to take care of themselves and are best steered into therapy.

Talking to Kids about Financial Challenges

Financial challenges often bring changes in lifestyle that can be met with resistance by one or more members of your family, including your partner. In many cases, these lifestyle changes were overdue. For example, our children today often feel entitled to having whatever they want, whenever they want it, regardless of our financial circumstances. As a result of our own unresolved money issues or childhood wounds, parents all too often succumb to their children's demands out of guilt, shame, frustration, or sheer fatigue. This is an enormous disservice to both the parent and the child. Children need to understand what the truth is and to learn that it is wise to live within one's means. If you model or teach them otherwise, they will most likely acquire negative and challenging money patterns as well. Do you and your partner really want this for your child? I don't believe you do.

Just because we're adults and parents does not mean that we always know what to say or do in these circumstances. Listen to your gut. If your child is acting out or is becoming increasingly demanding or showing an attitude of entitlement, this may be a symptom of other unmet needs or issues that need to be addressed. At the very least, these behaviors are a sign that you may need some help creating new guidelines and boundaries with your child.

When families are stretched financially, it may not be possible to give an allowance for chores. If this is the case in your family, simply explain to your children that as they get older, they get new responsibilities — that everyone in a family needs to pitch in and this is perfectly okay. Tell your children that doing household chores is a team effort and part of what it means to be a family. Here are some healthy reasons to empower your children to be members of your household team:

- It will provide them with a sense of competency.
- It will foster a sense of pride and self-confidence.

- It will teach them necessary life skills that they will carry into adulthood.
- It will teach them to be organized and more mindful of their time.
- It will help prevent them from developing entitlement issues, which are increasingly pervasive and problematic among the youth in our society.
- It will keep them from taking you, their parents, for granted.

Empowering Children to Help Out

I know it can be hard to ask the children in our lives to make sacrifices and to help out when times are tough and money is tight. But I think it can be *good* for them to pitch in and contribute to their own and the family's financial needs — within reason, of course. Here are some healthy reasons to encourage children (over the age of fourteen) to find ways to help out financially. Taking this approach will do the following:

- Empower them to know they can actually make money on their own
- Encourage them to be creative with their gifts and talents
- Increase their self-esteem
- Provide them with valuable life experience
- Keep them from feeling victimized by their circumstances
- Teach them the meaning and value of money

Finally, it is life altering for children to learn that if they truly want something, they have the capacity to find ways to earn and create it for themselves. That being said, children under fourteen are generally not permitted to work at a "real" job, nor should they be. Also, working should never interfere with a child's education. But there are things any young person can do after school to make money. Some good examples include dog walking, helping an elderly neighbor with chores, babysitting, simple gardening, lawn mowing, tutoring, running errands, being a personal assistant or mother's helper (for older teens with a car). Just make sure the "job" is safe and appropriate for your child's age and capacity.

Chapter Ten

CO-CREATING A RICH AND FINANCIALLY EMPOWERED RELATIONSHIP

To love means to open ourselves to the negative
as well as the positive — to grief, sorrow, and disappointment
as well as to joy, fulfillment, and an intensity of consciousness
we did not know was possible before.

— ROLLO MAY, *Love and Will*

I often ask couples that I work with to tell me what they believe would make them happy. Invariably, some will say, "We'd be happy if we were rich." Yet, when I probe a bit deeper and ask them to describe to me what "being rich" would look and feel like, almost every couple has a different picture. Clearly, what it means to be rich is subjective and has more to do with our deeper desire to be free and experience a more fully engaged life. Too many falsely believe that only the wealthy can afford to live their lives dedicated to the pursuit of their purpose, dreams, and personal happiness. This is true only if you believe it is.

If you believe that you cannot have or do *something* (*anything*, actually), then it is unfortunately a fait accompli, already your destiny. This is why I highly advise you to monitor your thoughts and suspend your disbelief, choosing instead to focus on creating what you want and believing that it is possible.

Although having a lot of money is useful on this human journey, I have found that with enough passion and determination, we are *all* capable of living a rich life, regardless of our financial circumstances. Over the years, I have met many people who have made an art out of living. These people are gifted in what I call the *art of living rich*. Their lives are tapestries of their own invention woven out of their passion for life and a commitment to doing what they love, being of service, expressing their gifts, and/or making a difference in the world. Some of the attitudes and attributes they have in common are a deep faith and belief in something bigger and greater than themselves; a vision that is mission and purpose based; and a deep passion for something that is meaningful to themselves, their families, or their communities. These people live in alignment with their values, and they never let *having* or *not having* money deter them from being or doing what they came here to do. Because these adventurous souls were so willing to move through life without a safety net, not only did they live rich lives, but sometimes they became wealthy as well. However, financial wealth was never their cause; rather, it was the *result* of their living intentionally and in alignment with their vision, values, and purpose. The wealth they acquired was a bonus for their efforts but inconsequential to their journey.

Cultivating a Rich Life

Living a rich life is quite different from being rich. Living rich is a state of mind and a way of being, not the state of your bank account. While you can always become rich by attaining more wealth, that is not a guarantee for manifesting a truly rich life.

Creating a truly rich life is not about having; it is about being. It is not something you can buy; it is something you become. We sometimes hear stories from our parents or grandparents about a single prized possession they had — a silver mirror, a beautiful set of china, a vintage car that they proudly polished on weekends. These were treasures that they cherished and enjoyed for years no matter how little money they had. It is unlikely that as they enjoyed these treasures, the owners were lamenting how little they had. They were absorbed in the joy of the moment. The treasures that make us feel wealthy may not even be material objects. A yearly vacation to the coast, visits across country to be with loved ones or friends, or just hanging out in the company of loved ones can also give us a sense of having and living a rich life.

I'd like to suggest that you give yourself more of whatever it is that allows you that expansive feeling of being wealthy and living a rich life. This usually has little to do with what you have or how much — it's about how the experience touches you and makes you feel connected to something larger than yourself. That is the secret of feeling and being truly "wealthy." When some part of your spirit is being reflected back to you by an experience, person, or object that you are enjoying, it is truly magical. Having more and more *things* will not give you that experience, nor will it make you truly wealthy. Landfills everywhere are full of broken toys and abandoned things that we once thought we needed. What we greatly need more of is to feel *engaged* with our passion, our purpose, and people to connect with and nourish our lives and spirit in ways that are *enriching*. When you and your partner discover what this is for you and allow yourselves to live and express more of this in your daily life, then together you will most certainly be wealthier.

Getting Started: Creating a New Vision for Your Life

As you go forward to create your rich life together, I encourage you to move in the direction of your hearts rather than your wallets, but to do so mindfully. I know plenty of wealthy people who are miserable and, conversely, others without wealth who live truly rich lives. It is essential that you understand that creating true wealth is first and foremost an *inside job. Whether you were born into poverty or with a silver spoon, there is no limit to what you can do, dream, learn, or become. So what are you waiting for?*

Be aware that there are certain risks in waiting before you jump-start your life. One very real risk is that it may never happen. Or by the time it does happen, you may have become overly comfortable not taking chances and too fearful to risk change. So, wherever you are in your lives together right now, this moment is the best time to begin taking the necessary steps toward creating a new vision for your life, personally and financially, that is both rich and rewarding. While there is no one way to do this, the exercises I've provided in this chapter are an excellent place to get started. Give yourselves an afternoon or even a full day to complete this process together. It is an investment in your lives, and I promise you that doing so will be fun and inspiring and will bring you closer. Use your journals as you work through these exercises. Write down your thoughts and feelings as they surface. May doing this work lead you to the rediscovery of a dream that you may have misplaced or reconnect you to a passion that you both still long to have fulfilled. Let your imagination run free, and discover where it might lead you.

Creating Your Rich Life Road Map — Begin Where You Are

To create a rich and financially empowered life together, you first need to be clear about where you are and what you need for the journey. Below are some steps to take to get started:

STEP ONE. Start with a large white posterboard; draw a red dot on it and write "We Are Here"; and glue a photo of yourselves and your family, if you have children (or pets!). Put your posterboard to the side for now — you will need it later for another exercise in the book.

STEP TWO. On a separate piece of paper, write down everything in your lives that is working well, personally and financially. You can use your gratitude lists, created earlier, to help you get started. Don't forget to include where you are financially — how much income do you bring in together each month, what are your expenses, what is your financial net worth? Spend time together looking at where you are, personally and financially. It's essential to understand where you are, financially speaking, so that you can figure out how to get where you're going. The writer and philosopher Ayn Rand wrote, "Money is only a tool. It will take you wherever you wish, but it will not replace you as the driver." From a money coaching point of view, this could not be truer. All the money in the world will not take you where you want to go if you aren't in control of your own patterns and behaviors and you continue to drive into the same potholes year after year. Being or becoming wealthy is one thing; learning how to consciously *be with money* is quite another. Money is a means, but without the right driver in the driver's seat, few people arrive where they hoped they'd be. It is up to you to become the drivers of your own dreams!

STEP THREE. Answer the following questions:

1. Which money types are driving your financial life?
2. Which one of you is behind the wheel? Or is one of

you the designated driver because the other doesn't feel as comfortable, or perhaps competent, as you?

3. What's preventing either of you from being a fully empowered financial driver or co-pilot in your life?

4. If you suddenly won the lottery, would either of you be prepared to manage the road ahead to your new wealth?

5. Imagine that you've just discovered you are holding a winning lottery ticket worth $3 million. Before you cash in your prize, you must present your plan to the lottery ticket office for approval. Write down what you plan to do with the money and the impact this will have on your lives.

Activating the Perfect Money Types

Belief in the "perfection" of the number three and things in three has been passed down through the ages. The Latin phrase *omne trinum perfectum* means "all things in three are perfect." This also holds true in the forming of the perfect money type configuration. When working with clients, I look to help people to build and strengthen their Warrior, Magician, and Creator/Artist aspects because together they represent the most powerful combination of archetypes.

The Warrior is the archetype of action, and as such, it is the aspect you will need for implementing your vision. The Warrior has the focus, discipline, and determination to get you to your desired destination. Thus, the Warrior is always the best archetype to put in charge as the driver.

Even with a good map as our guide, sometimes the road ahead can become foggy and unclear. This requires the faith and trust of the Magician, as co-pilot, who holds the key to the unseen world and will serve as your guide and compass should the road ahead become uncertain or unclear.

And finally, you will need the Creator/Artist to inspire and help you to create your life's vision and purpose. The Creator/Artist within us serves as our constant companion and guide and will provide you with inspiration and creativity on your journey.

As for your more challenging money types, such as the Innocent, Victim, Fool, Martyr, and Tyrant, let's just say that it is best to keep these characters in the trunk! Periodically take them to the beach and let them play a while, but never let them drive your financial life, as they tend to cause unnecessary challenges and may sabotage your efforts to arrive at your destination.

EXERCISE

Envisioning Your Life: Begin with the End in Mind

Now that you know where you are and who's driving the car, it's time to envision where you want to be when you arrive. After all, if you don't know what it looks like, how will you recognize it? The purpose of this visioning exercise is to help you to gain clarity about the life you desire to create as you move forward. Begin this process with the end in mind.

Both of you close your eyes and imagine that you are walking along a magnificent riverbank on a beautiful, sunny day. You are excited about your new life together. You feel happy and purposeful and trust that all is unfolding perfectly. Suddenly, a red rowboat appears out of nowhere and invites you to come aboard. You feel no fear or resistance and calmly step inside the boat, which has no oars, certain that it will take you to your destiny.

As you ride down the river, the warm sun makes you sleepy, and you decide to lie down and rest. The boat gently rocks you into a deep sleep, the deepest sleep you have ever known. While sleeping, you dream about the life you have hoped for and worked toward for many years. When you awaken, ten years have passed. The boat has landed on an embankment, and you step out to discover that you have arrived exactly where you always hoped for and envisioned. All of your efforts, visioning, planning, and dreams have been realized. Answer these questions in your journal.

- Where are you, and what are you doing together?
- How has your life together evolved?
- What rewards have you received for your journey?
- How did you know when you had arrived?

Now, describe to each other the life that each of you has envisioned creating for yourselves. If what you have envisioned is quite different (which is not unusual), work together to merge the best of what you've each envisioned into a shared vision, so you can begin to co-create what you both truly desire.

Launching Your Vision and Purpose

Now that you have properly envisioned your life, it is important to move beyond any real or perceived blocks or limitations to creating your new reality. Manifesting anything requires creativity and commitment, which are essential ingredients to changing lifelong habits and beliefs that often keep us stuck. Commitment is essential because change does not just magically happen. Creativity is necessary because all change requires a new level of awareness, and *everything new begins in the imagination.* So if you want to change your life and manifest greater abundance, you will need to become inspired and use what Spirit has given you creatively — and yes, even *differently* than you may have in the past. This might also require a commitment to changing how you think, act, and speak on a daily basis.

Anchoring Your Vision through Prayer, Affirmations, and Intentions

A wonderful way to stay grounded and connected to your life's vision is to anchor it daily through intentional prayer and/or affirmations. The purpose of your prayer or affirmations is to create and work *your specific intentions* for the life you wish to create together. Your intentions represent your mutual hopes, desires, and dreams. Each sentence is an affirmative statement of a goal, outcome, or circumstance you are intending to create. The key to this process of intention is to create statements or affirmations that are in alignment with the purpose, mission, and vision you hold for your life together. Be specific and always make your statements in the present tense. Focus your intentions on the highest good of your relationship and family. Here is an example:

Affirmation for Creating Financial Intimacy

We honor this relationship and know that our love is the sacred home of our heart.

Nothing is more important than this home, and we vow to do everything to protect and support this bond between us.

We consciously choose love, kindness, and generosity to guide our thoughts and actions.

We use money as a means of providing for our true wants and needs.

We are committed to co-creating a life that is in alignment with our true values.

We are good and able financial stewards, and we use our
   resources wisely.
We honor and respect money as a blessing that we receive
   in gratitude.
We experience our lives from a place of abundance.
Together, we are manifesting our vision, intention, and
   purpose with ease and grace. And so it is.

Manifestation Collage

Now that you have created your vision and intentions together,
it is time to put this into a visual framework by doing a "manifestation collage." Go back to the large posterboard that you set
up earlier, and begin to create your manifestation collage in the
image that visually depicts all that you seek to manifest in your
life. Focus on the specific aspects of your life that you now know
you intend to create, personally and financially. For instance, if
you would like a new home, find photographs of a home that
represents the kind of home you'd both like to live in. Not just
any home, but one that has the style, feel, look, and aspects of the
new home that you both desire. The key is to make your manifestation collage look as much as possible like the vision you have
worked together to develop. The more specifically your collage
visually represents your desired outcome, the easier it will be to
manifest. Include words and images that depict the life and lifestyle you both desire in all areas of your life: health, happiness,
right livelihood, family, and spirituality. Cut out and paste words,
phrases, and images from magazines and add family photos to
your collage board that reflect each of these specific areas. Be sure
to focus only on what you want to create. Each picture, word,
phrase, and image needs to properly reflect your intention and
desire. Do not include anything you don't truly wish to create.

The manifestation collage is a great process to help you to consciously co-create the rich and empowered life you seek to build together. Once you've completed it, have it laminated and place it somewhere in your home along with your intentions. Work your prayer or affirmations on a daily basis, and begin to notice how your own inner work, commitment, and actions begin to reshape your reality.

Creating Your Life Plan and Strategy

Next, you will need to come up with a specific plan and strategy for building the life you have envisioned. Your plan involves becoming clear about *what* you need to do, and your strategy involves determining *how* to best achieve it. The Warrior knows that without a good plan and strategy, our vision cannot be moved into a reality.

Here is the formula for manifesting your vision:

CLARITY OF VISION + PURPOSE + INTENTION
+ FOCUSED INTENTION + RIGHT ACTION
+ COMMITMENT + FAITH + TRUST
= MANIFESTATION OF YOUR NEW REALITY

EXERCISE

Your Plan and Strategy

Take everything you have worked on in this chapter and put it into this template. Simply write the following sentences in your money coaching journal and fill in the blanks:

Together, we have clarified the new vision for our life. Our vision is _____.

Our collective purpose is _____
_____.

Our specific intentions are _____
_____.

Our attention will be focused on _____
_____.

We are committed to doing these daily right actions:
_____.

We commit to doing a daily spiritual practice that
involves _____.

We put our faith in _____ and trust that
all is unfolding perfectly for our highest good.

As you proceed into the future, allow your Creator/Artist to provide you with creativity, inspiration, and vision. Call on your Warrior to implement your vision and intentions through focused attention and daily right action. And ask your Magician to help you to stay aligned with your higher purpose and soul's intention, to hold this together in balance. Your inner Magician will help you both to stay awake and aware of old patterns that no longer serve you and need to be healed and transformed. Together, these represent your power archetypes that, when balanced and in harmony, have the greatest capacity to help you to manifest the rich and financially empowered life you envision together. Over time, as you continue to do this work, you will begin to master both the inner and outer worlds, integrating the material with the spiritual, in which you realize that all of life is sacred and connected to the Source.

Creating financial intimacy is a process, not a journey. Intimacy is created through the process of learning how to be vulnerable and to trust deeply. To be worthy of that trust, you both must be willing to commit to creating a field of emotional safety between you in which your innermost selves can fully show up to be seen and heard. In this space between you, agree to welcome each other into any money conversation, no matter how challenging or difficult. Remember, conversations about money may still be emotionally triggering at times, so use the healthy communication tools you've learned in this book. When you engage in money discussions, notice which of your money types are present in the conversation. If one of your more challenging types is leading the conversation, consciously choose one of your more positive archetypes to step into the conversation. Should you find yourselves in a conflict, agree to take a time-out, spend some time in quiet reflection rather than reaction, and agree to resume the conversation later.

Learn to treat the intimacy between you like an exquisite piece of fine crystal: solid and strong at its core, but fragile if not handled with care. Acknowledge your efforts as you move forward and begin to transform the patterns and behaviors that no longer serve you, and commit to building those that do. Respect, love, and honor the journey you are on together, and know that with faith and trust, all will unfold in time. May the richness that you discover be filled with treasures from both the inner and outer worlds. May your love and financial intimacy blossom more fully with each day.

NOTES

Chapter One. Money: The Last Taboo

Page 2, *a taboo is "something that is avoided or forbidden"*: Cambridge Dictionary (Cambridge, England: Cambridge University Press, 2011).

Page 3, *Carl Jung wrote that "everyone carries a shadow"*: C. G. Jung, *Psychology and Religion* (New Haven: Yale University Press, 1938), 93.

Page 6, *"Every word, facial expression, gesture, or action"*: Virginia Satir, *The New Peoplemaking* (Palo Alto, CA: Science and Behavior Books, 1988), 25.

Page 7, *nine out of ten lottery winners spend or lose all their winnings within five years*: Don McNay, quoted in John Seewer, "Mega Millions Jackpot: What to Do after You Win," *Huffington Post*, March 29, 2012, www.huffingtonpost.com/2012/03/29/mega-millions-jackpot-winner_n_1389763.html.

Page 9, *the phenomenon first identified by Donald Hebb, a Canadian neuropsychologist*: Donald Hebb, *The Organization of Behavior: A Neuropsychological Theory* (New York: John Wiley & Sons, 1949).

Chapter Three. Yours, Mine, and Ours: Money Patterns

Page 33, *this cycle, known as the* hedonic treadmill: The term *hedonic treadmill* was coined by Philip Brickman and Donald T. Campbell in their essay "Hedonic Relativism and Planning the Good Society," in *Adaptation Level Theory: A Symposium*, ed. Mortimer Herbert Appley (New York: Academic Press, 1971), 287–302.

Chapter Five. Managing Your Money Conversations

Page 89, *For Bohm, "Consciousness...involves awareness"*: David Bohm, *Wholeness and the Implicate Order* (1980; reprint, London: Routledge, 2005), 251–52.

Page 92, *one definition of the word* appreciation: *American Heritage Dictionary of the English Language*, 4th ed. (Boston: Houghton Mifflin, 2000).

Chapter Seven. Overcoming Financial Challenges and Setbacks

Page 123, *Here is a beautiful poem called "Prayer" by Charles Elkind*: Charles Elkind, "Prayer," www.charliescards.com/poetrypage3 .html. Used with permission.

Page 126, *According to a 2010 report of the Federal Reserve Bank*: *The Survey of Consumer Payment Choice*, Federal Reserve Bank of Boston, January 2010.

Chapter Ten. Co-creating a Rich and Financially Empowered Relationship

Page 169, *Ayn Rand wrote, "Money is only a tool"*: Ayn Rand, *Atlas Shrugged* (1957; reprint, New York: Plume, 1999), 411.

RESOURCES

Financial Education

Money coaching and Certified Money Coach (CMC) Training: www.MoneyCoachingInstitute.com

National Endowment for Financial Education: www.nefe.org

Financial Planning Association: www.fpanet.org

U.S. Securities and Exchange Commission: www.sec.gov

Financial Industry Regulatory Association:
www.finra.org/Investors/ProtectYourself

Credit Counseling and Education

Association for Financial Counseling, Planning and Education: www.afcpe.org

National Foundation for Credit Counseling: www.nfcc.org

CERTIFIED MONEY COACHES

Locate a Certified Money Coach (CMC)® trained specifically in the Heart of Money Coaching Process for Couples in your area. (Note: Many of the coaches listed here also work with clients remotely.)

Northern California

Cotati

ROBERTA HOLLEMAN
(707) 494-1296
www.symbaservices.com
robertaholleman@gmail.com

Marin/Novato

KAREN HARVEY
(415) 884-9265
www.innerwealthwisdom.com
karen@innerwealthwisdom.com

DEBORAH PRICE
(415) 895-1069
www.moneycoachinginstitute.com
dprice@money-therapy.com

Modesto

LYNN TELFORD-SAHL
(209) 492-8745
www.lynntelfordsahl.com
lynntelfordsahl@gmail.com

San Francisco

MEGAN LATHROP COX
(415) 307-3575
http://fa.ml.com/theduffygroup
meganlathropcox@gmail.com

Santa Rosa

ANGIE M. GRAINGER
(707) 528-4465
www.49secretsofmoney.com
Angie.Grainger@rethinkmoney
    coaching.com

Seaside

JULIA ARZE MERCADO
(831) 917-2837
www.juliaarze.com
juliaarze@yahoo.com

Sonoma

DONNA COLFER
(707) 484-4246
www.buildingwealthfrom
    within.com
donna@buildingwealthfrom
    within.com

Walnut Creek

STEVEN SHAGRIN
(925) 949-3938
www.planningforlife.info
Shags@planningforlife.info

Southern California

Agoura

ALECIA CAINE
(805) 218-1277
www.moneychi.com
abccpa@sbcglobal.net

Culver City

MICHAEL LAINE
(310) 568-4516
www.mlaine.net
michael.laine@lpl.com

BRENDA HOLLAND PAGE
(310) 746-0524
www.innerconnections
    coaching.com
bpobrenda@gmail.com

Santa Barbara

CECILE LYONS
(805) 845-4755
ckplyons@gmail.com

Thousand Oaks

TRACY WILLIAMS
(323) 791-2533
www.youaremoneysmart.com
info@youaremoneysmart.com

West Los Angeles

DR. SANDY PLONE
(310) 979-7473
dr.plone@verizon.net

Georgia

DR. LORRAINE EDEY
Jasper, GA
(321) 288-0692
www.coachinginspirations.com
loridey@aol.com

New York

LESLIE STREBEL
Ithaca, NY
(607) 275-1275
www.strebelcpa.com
leslie@strebelcpa.com

Virginia

YU-FEN CHANG-PETT
Paris, VA
(540) 877-6221
www.moneywisdom
   empowerment.com
moneywisdomempowerment
   @gmail.com

Australia

Melbourne (Somerville)

JENNIE NEWLAND
(61) 0409 238 882
jennie@anewland.com.au

Sydney and Tasmania

JANE HORN
(61) 0400 202 716
www.rivetfinancial.com.au
jane@rivetfinancial.com.au

Bolivia

JULIA ARZE MERCADO
Cochabamba
(591) 44660066
www.juliaarze.com
Juliaarze@yahoo.com

Canada

SUE HUTCHINSON BAWDEN
Fernie, British Columbia
(250) 423-6697
www.evolveinkcoaching.com
sue@evolveinkcoaching.com

England

HELEN COLLIER
Menston, West Yorkshire
(44) 01943 874765
www.harmoneylife.co.uk
helen@harmoneylife.co.uk

Indonesia

BRENDA FERREIRA
Ubud, Bali
(62) 0818 05 344 309
www.brendaferreira.com
brendaferr@gmail.com

Malaysia

FLORENCE LAM
Kuala Lumpur
(60) 122899833
www.moneyawakening.com
florencelam2u@gmail.com

Singapore

JOAN SWEE
Singapore
(65) 95847715
joan@jsconsultrain.com

ERNEST TAN
Singapore
(65) 31509318
www.jopezacademy.com
jopezacademy@gmail.com

INDEX

ABOUT THE AUTHOR

Deborah Price is a money coach and the founder and CEO of the Money Coaching Institute, which provides money coaching, consulting, and coach training to individuals, couples, and businesses. An international speaker, consultant, and trainer, she has trained hundreds of coaches and other professionals around the world. A former financial adviser for over twenty years with firms such as Merrill Lynch, MassMutual, AIG, and London Pacific Advisors, Deborah left the financial industry in 2000 to pioneer the field of money coaching. Money coaching is a step-by-step process for identifying and changing unconscious money patterns, beliefs, and behaviors in order to live a more purposeful and financially conscious life.

She is the author of *Money Magic: Unleashing Your True Potential for Prosperity and Fulfillment* (originally published in hardcover under the title *Money Therapy*) and *Start Investing Online Today!* She is working on a new book called *Family Money: Creating and Sustaining a Legacy of Love and Wealth*. A leading expert in her field, Deborah has appeared on numerous radio and television shows around the world. She resides in Northern California with her husband, Robert, and daughter, Anjelica.